Welcome to the Houseboat

Santee Map Left Panel

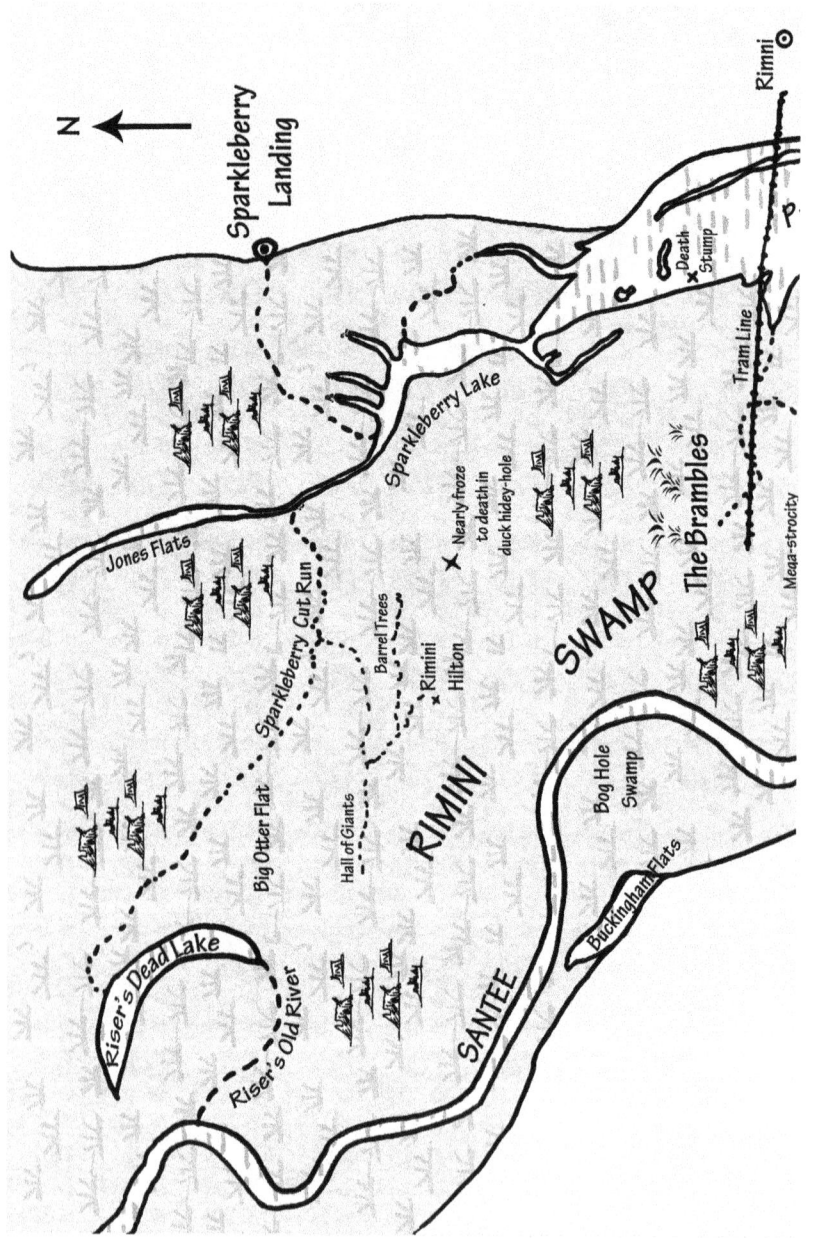

Santee Map Right Panel

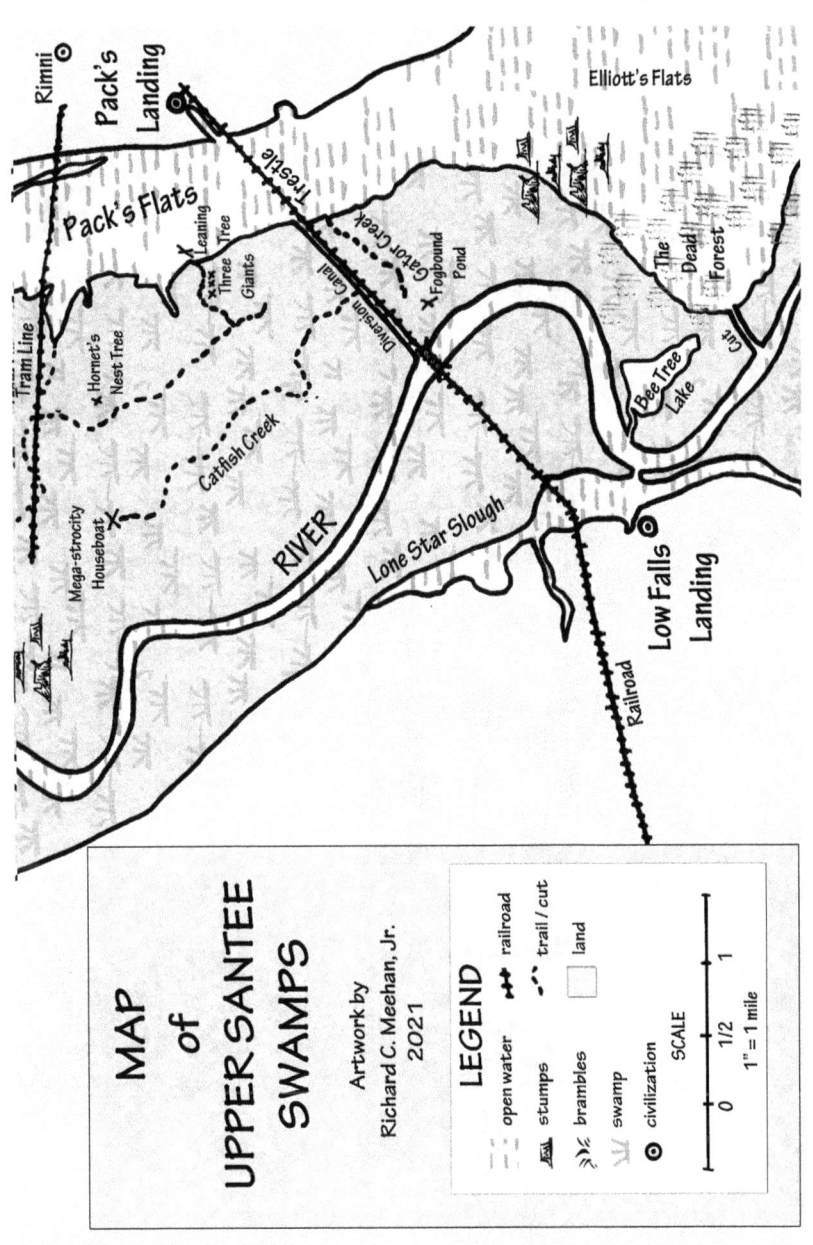

Santee, Wilderness Wonderland

Laugh With The Ducks

Duck Tale

Duck Tale

MEMOIR OF A QUACKING GOOD TREK TO MANHOOD

Richard C. Meehan, Jr.

Noggin Universe Press, LLC

Copyright © 2021 Richard C. Meehan, Jr.

All rights reserved. No part of this book may be reproduced in any form or by any electronic or mechanical means, including information storage and retrieval systems, without permission in writing from the publisher, except by reviewers, who may quote brief passages in a review.

Library of Congress Control Number: 2021910954

Most illustrations and photos were created or taken by the author. Other images are credited to the contributor in captions.

Laughing Duck line drawing by Douglas R. Meehan.

Printed in the United States of America
First Edition

ISBN-13: 978-1-7372975-0-5 (hardcover)
ISBN-10: 1-73729-750-7 (hardcover)

Published by Noggin Universe Press, Spartanburg, South Carolina.
www.nogginuniverse.com
info@nogginuniverse.com

Visit https://www.rcmeehan.com for more about this author.

I dedicate these stories to my family that they may recall a little of the wisdom of one

RICHARD "DICK" CARL MEEHAN,

grandfather, father, hunter, and friend.

Disclaimer

At the time of this writing some of the characters herein have passed away. While these events really happened, the exact conversations of the people have since dispersed into the mind's oblivion; therefore, the narrative is a compilation of many such dialogues that occurred over a lengthy period.

Maps are included for illustration only, not for orienteering. Neither the author nor the publisher expresses or implies that using this information will prepare anyone for a visit to Santee. As with all excursions into wilderness areas, Santee can be dangerous even to an experienced visitor.

Contents

Dedication   xi
Disclaimer   xiii

1	Introduction	1
2	Sting	6
3	Dead Forest	23
4	Shades of Gray	39
5	To Hunt or Not	51
6	Another Big Day	71
7	Death Stump	81
8	Barrel Hunters	95
9	Duck Dog	102
10	One Good Turn	109
11	Deserves Another	117
12	Toy	130
13	One Starry Night	142
14	Resurrection	150
15	The Redo	157

16	Various and Sundry	164
17	What Now?	174
18	Dudes	183
19	Under the Influence	200
20	Pack Rat	206
21	Diorama	214
22	Pop's Farewell	222

Appendix	225
Acknowledgments	251
Also Available	253
About The Author	254
In Remembrance	256
Parts Of The Boat	257

At first the strikes were temperate, but they grew harder. Why is each stroke a cannon blast in my ears? Doesn't he hear me? Wake up, Pop. WAKE UP!

1

Introduction

Witnessing a loved one die is hard. I don't know if there's anything else in the world that comes close to the devastation you feel as life slips away before you. In my case, it was my father – Pop. As real men approach all aspects of life, Pop went into the Beyond with a reserved sort of violence. He put up a fight to live that spanned more than two years but finally succumbed to the ravages of leukemia. He took it like a man.

Man. What a misunderstood word! At what point does a boy become a man? Is it when he turns twenty-one? Could it be on Graduation Day? Perhaps it comes with the birth of his first child? The answer: None of the above. Manhood is a state of mind, pure and simple. It is an achievement culled from mistakes and triumphs. Age has nothing to do with it.

Boy. Kid. Son. Pick any one of those titles interchangeably, and that's what Pop used to call me. As the occasion warranted, he'd call me other things too. On that final afternoon of October 2, 1991, as I slapped Pop's face, hoping he would open his eyes once more, I fully expected him to wake up and hit me back. It was the only time in my life that I lost control of myself and struck him. I wasn't angry. I was desperate – begging for one more moment of his attention. With each blow, all the good times paraded across my mind, times that I chose to forget while he was alive. His goal was to teach me how to be a man. We were at odds most of the time.

As a boy, I did not understand the extraordinary value and importance of the time-sacrifices Pop made for me. "Good times" were when he could be outdoors, especially when hunting season came along, no matter the weather. It seemed as if I was no more than a tag-a-long, useful only as a gofer. Always "going for" stuff made me angry, so I tried to reduce Pop's enjoyment of hunting on occasion by acting like a two-year-old. At the time, I had no children of my own. A few years later, I got it. Believe me.

Most everyone fashions an emotional jail, a comfortable box inside our heads decorated with security, power, and control. Pop's cage was also physical. Marko, Inc., his janitorial outfit in Spartanburg, South Carolina, was his own custom-designed, time-stealing pokey. Since he was the boss, the Head Honcho, the Responsible

Duck Tale

Party, and as one employee was fond of calling him, "Cap'n," getting away from Marko was a real treat. On those occasions when Pop cut his self-made shackles loose, Hunting was the reason. If it flew and was a legal game bird, Pop hunted it. From dove, duck, turkey, quail, grouse, pheasant, goose, and marsh hen, Pop spent every spare moment during the season where the birds were. So, I spent much time doing the same thing. I didn't appreciate it then. Now I wish I could repeat every second – even the time I nearly froze to death in an iced-over swamp down at Santee.

The lower part of the Palmetto State is full of swamps and marshes, a waterfowler's paradise. Consequently, my father and I spent much time around Pack's Flats, Lake Marion's northernmost

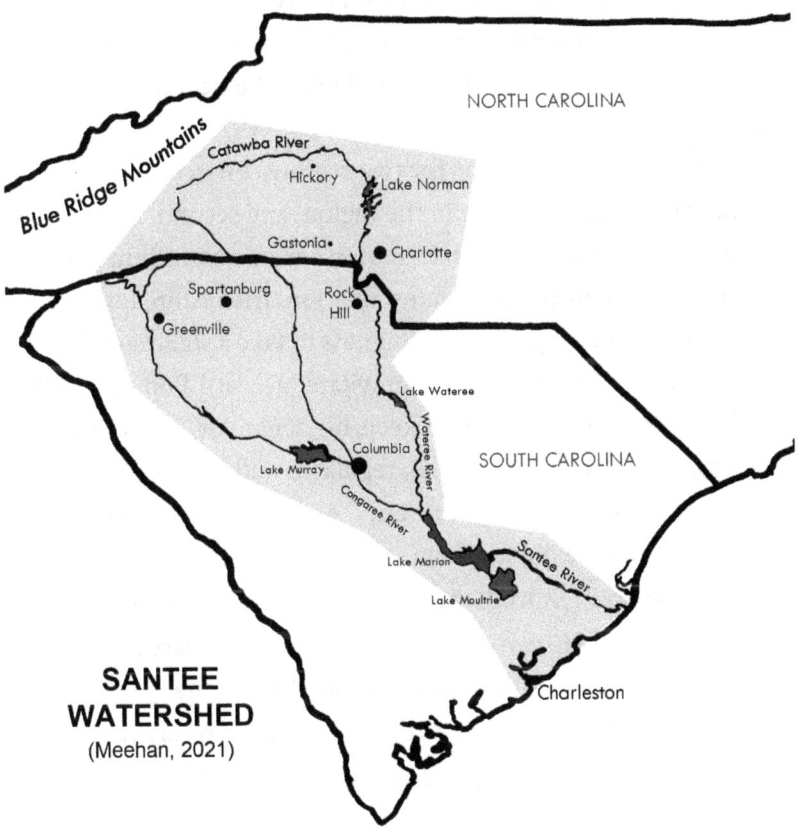

area. South toward Charleston and Georgetown's coastal regions is a wildlife refuge teeming with fish, amphibians, reptiles, birds, and mammals. The Santee River Basin, as this region is known, was useful long before my time.

During the Revolutionary War, Colonel Francis Marion, a.k.a. the Swamp Fox, commander of the Second South Carolina Regiment, left the British forces of Lt. Col. "Bloody Ban" Banastre Tarleton bewildered. The British soldiers tried to track the Swamp Fox and his Patriots through the dark, mosquito-infested cypress wilderness. But Marion's forces used guerrilla warfare tactics. The Patriots would fade in and out of the Santee to raid British strongholds with impunity and disappear. Tarleton led his cavalry from Charleston to pursue Marion through twenty-six miles of the swamp. Finally, the infamous British colonel gave up the pursuit and declared, "But as for this damn old fox, the devil himself could not catch him."

I mention the Swamp Fox for two reasons. First, to illustrate the area people's historical pride in the region, and second, Marion and my father shared similar traits. Marion's men saw in him some of the qualities Pop displayed – determination, friendship, love, devotion, support, fair play, and a willingness to take a stance on the side of righteousness. Men naturally gravitated toward Pop. Like Marion, Pop relentlessly fought to keep his regiment, i.e., the family business, alive. To this day, folks regularly walk up to me and say, "I knew your dad. He was a great guy." A short story usually follows about something he did for them.

As a true leader, my father *cared*. He cared about people. He cared about God. He cared about the country. He cared about our family. He cared about his friends. He cared about me.

A man stands for what he believes is *right*. Pop told me on numerous occasions, "If you know you are in the right, don't let anyone or anything stand in your way." He believed he was right to drag me along on all those hunting trips with his buddies, and he was, but I didn't know it then. I just took pleasure in tormenting him by trying to make him think I hated it. Time changes many things.

My own son and daughter are both grown now. There was nothing easy about raising them; I doubt any parent finds childrearing easy. After all, no formula works for every child. I think the best any parent can hope for is that their children grow up to be good people, on the side of Light. There is far too much Darkness in the world already. My father's method of raising a son to manhood was to offer the path through a combination of Christianity, nature appreciation, education, and hard work. I believe Pop succeeded, and while I can't tell him to his face right now, I will have a chance in the Life Hereafter.

There are many rough patches on the road to manhood. Some are humorous, some embarrassing, and a few downright abusive to the psyche – like witnessing the death of a loved one. No matter what fell onto my plate, Pop insisted that I learned not to complain. The words "take it like a man" would sometimes filter into his advice. The answer to navigating challenging situations was to "keep putting one foot in front of the other." If tears came, well, okay, "but don't keep wallowing in the pigpen." Life does go on. Along the way, the psyche either grows or withers. The trick is to learn new coping methods like I began to do one day so long ago....

"The gem cannot be polished without friction, nor man perfected without trials."
~ Chinese Proverb

Sting

"Open the cooler, open the cooler!" My father's rich bellow steamrolled across the watery expanse. I turned from my panoramic view to see him wiggling through the bait shop's screen door with two twenty-pound bags of ice. He wore a white tee shirt and Korean War surplus camouflaged pants in brown, olive green, and khaki blobs. Atop his head rode a matching ball cap with duck feathers poking from some of the vent holes. Black hair stuck out around the cap's base, much like the copious uni-brow above his black-framed lenses. The glasses were thick, concentrating the cobalt blue of his eyes into focused lasers. A combination of John Wayne and Andy Griffith, Pop was bearing down on his friend, Vernon "Vee Bee" Burnett.

"Hold yer horses, Dick!" Squat and round, Mr. Burnett struggled to remove the second of two large coolers from the back of our new Tar Heel Blue '68 Chevy Station Wagon. He, too, was garbed in camouflage.

"Boy! Don't just stand there! Get over here and give Vee Bee a hand!" Pop was six-foot-four, two hundred forty-two pounds of mostly muscle. Did I mention loud? When he whispered, a crowded room could hear every syllable. Sometimes I found it embarrassing. He seemed to take great pleasure in keeping me in a state of mortification – such as now. Even the gnats swarming high above seemed buffeted by the sound waves Pop emanated.

Immediately I crossed the graveled launch from my formerly quiet vantage, a small knoll to the left of the boat ramp. I jockeyed around Mr. Burnett, positioning myself to grab one handle of the cooler in both hands. My skinny body protested as I lifted, yet the heavy aluminum cooler eased to the ground after clipping the car's bumper only once, on my end, of course.

"Where's your muscle, Boy?" crowed Pop. "Get that lid open, Vee Bee!"

Mr. Burnett huffed, puffed, and twisted the latch of the cooler to throw open the lid just as both bags of ice came crashing down on top of the cans, bottles, and food. I barely got my fingers out of the way in time to keep them from getting crushed.

"Watch your fingers, Boy! Tear this bag open and fill the other cooler too. You want cold drinks, don't you?" Pop never missed a thing.

"Yes, sir." I knew it was customary to call elders, anyone older than myself, Sir, Mister, Ma'am, Misses, or Miss. Pop said it was a sign of respect, but it could be tiresome. Since leaving home, I'd said it at least a hundred times already – and the weekend was only just getting started.

"When you get finished with that, go stand back out of the way!" He spun around and stalked to the driver's side of the car.

"Yes, sir." I cupped my hands and began to shovel ice between the coolers. They turned stiff and red and started to ache. I noticed myself looking down at the top of Mr. Burnett's cap, a plain tan one. Surprised, I realized I must have grown some lately. Since he was freezing his own hands without complaint, I decided not to mention the cold either.

"Got these coolers from the Pepsi plant the other day, Ricky," said Mr. Burnett. "They're *real* nice, ain't they?"

Not knowing what else to say to an adult, I replied, "Yes, sir."

"Management gave 'em to us maintenance men that'd been around more 'n ten years. Employee gifts, they called 'em. Quality made, too. Sheet metal, chrome latches. Bet they'll keep the ice frozen all weekend long."

"That's great, sir." I knew that Mr. Burnett worked at the Pepsi Cola Bottling Company in Spartanburg. These coolers were painted blue with the Pepsi logo in white. I couldn't help noticing there were lots of glass bottles of Pepsi in them too. At home, sodas were a rare treat. My mouth watered.

"Better get on back over there, now," said Mr. Burnett, his gray-blue eyes smiling from beneath his silver-framed spectacles. Beads of sweat moistened his sideburns. "You can warm yer hands back up by shaking 'em for a bit."

"Yes, sir." I returned to the knoll and tried to recapture my earlier musing. My hands did warm when I shook them, but that brought on a burning sensation in the knuckles. I gritted my teeth against the discomfort and forced myself to take in the view.

There was a strip of water about a quarter of a mile wide, almost like a thin lake. Moss-draped trees lined the opposite side. Directly before me was a gap in the trees through which I could see the moving water of the Santee River. Ever since we had arrived, flat-bottomed boats had been roaring in and out of this cut-through. Their passage filled the air with the greasy odor of outboard motor exhaust. It occurred to me that what I was seeing was the flooded riverbank, and these boats were coming and going between the river and the landing.

My eyes traveled upstream to my left and fell upon something I had not noticed earlier. Beneath a clump of cypress trees floated the houseboat. For months, I had watched this shanty rise from nothing in Mr. Burnett's yard. Excitement drove all thoughts of cold hands from my mind.

The houseboat looked like a thumb-sized utility building with an extended front stoop and an overhanging flat roof from this distance. It was constructed of marine plywood, painted grayish brown, which passed for camouflage. For half a year of weekends and evenings, my father and his friends had labored to build it. At last, the homemade construct was floating – a testament to human ingenuity. Pop told me that one could achieve anything he sets his mind to, and here bobbed the proof!

Behind me sat the bait shop and convenience store that comprised Low Falls Landing. It was the last stop for gasoline, oil, beer, snacks, bait, and ice before entering the world of black water and mossy cypress forests in the Santee River Basin of downstate South Carolina. Ahead of me was an unknown quantity, a promise of unique experiences. I gave a start, abruptly realizing someone was watching me.

Shielding my eyes against the midday sun, I could make out two people sitting on the houseboat's porch. Although I couldn't see their faces, I knew them to be two of Pop's other friends, Charlie Weathers and Don Libner. Their olive-green jon boat was tied off to the porch by some unseen tether. Both men were waving and pointing at me. I waved back, but then my gaze trailed further up the waterway. More houseboats of similar design were tied off to similar cypress clumps and surrounded by similar drifting masses of pigweed.

Noises made by Pop and Mr. Burnett began to encroach on my observations. I turned to see them bustling around our jon boat. Pop caught me looking.

"What're you doing, Boy? Get on down here and give us a hand!"

"Yes, sir," I called as I hustled over. Upon arrival, I found myself tossed up on the bow of the boat with camping paraphernalia coming my way.

"Here, catch!"

A large brown sleeping bag, an old WWII army surplus type insulated with pounds of goose down and as tall as me, nearly thumped me off my perch. It was all I could do to wrap my arms around it.

"Don't just stand there. Stow my bag and grab some more!"

"Heh, heh, heh," added Mr. Burnett.

The two of them reminded me of my favorite Hanna-Barbara cartoon characters, Fred Flintstone and Barney Rubble, two best friends from the Stone Age.

For the next ten minutes, I acted as a porter to the deluge of camping gear, cooking gear, boat gear, fishing gear, groceries, and tools. Once done, I had to crawl on top of the pile to get back to the bow.

Duck Tale

The Houseboat

Pigweed is a nickname plastered on several varieties of extremely invasive water plants clogging the Upper Lake of Santee Cooper. Varieties include hydrilla, elodea, and water hyacinth. Pigweed is like lily pads in that it is green, has leaves, and floats. That is where the similarities end. These invasive drifting masses are everywhere you look, much like kudzu on the land, hogging the natural waterways except where the water flow is swiftest. Spoiler alert: you never find frogs sitting on the leaves, only huge dragonflies, but you do have to keep clearing the prop of your outboard motor every so often to remove the tangled, ropy vines. Otherwise, pigweed will bring your boat to a standstill at the most inappropriate time.

"Here, grab onto this, and don't let go!" The end of a hemp rope slapped me on the cheek. I duly caught it and held on.

"Dick, don't ya think da boat's too full?"

"Hell, Vee Bee, don't be a Don't-bee, be a Do-bee. The boat will take it." Pop lumbered up to me as I looked down at him from my perch. "The Boy won't let it float away. Will you, Boy?" In a stage whisper that anyone could hear for miles, he said, "You hold on tight, now. Don't let it float away."

"Yes, sir," my high-pitched voice revealed my nervousness. After all, this was a first-time Big Deal. Besides, my brain was stuck on the words *float away*. I wondered if my eight-year-old wisp of a body had the strength to keep the overloaded boat from *floating away*.

On the three-hour trip down, I had heard Pop and Mr. Burnett saying that Santee Cooper was full of stumps that could punch through the bottom of a boat in a heartbeat. As yet, I couldn't visualize any of those hazards. They were simply lurking, weighing down my feelings as I watched Pop release the trailer hook to unfetter the boat. All too soon, the station wagon roared, its eight cylinders blasting clouds of white leaded gasoline smoke from its tailpipe. How would it feel to hit an unseen object while riding in a fourteen-foot-long aluminum boat?

Mr. Burnett, in his rumbling baritone voice, said, "You okay, Ricky? You're lookin' a tad peaked." I noticed that his chubby face held some of the same concern that I was feeling. "Don't worry. Jus' don't let go o' th' rope. I've got the other end." He looked over his shoulder and yelled, "Bring 'er on back, Dick!" then stepped to the side as the station wagon began to roll slowly backward. The transom of the boat hit the water, and gallons poured in. From my roost atop the pile of gear, it looked as if the boat was going to fill up, but it began to float.

"Stop, Dick! STOP!" Mr. Burnett shouted.

The car skidded to a halt. Muddy water sloshed through the open tailgate up to the middle seat. I could hear the *blub-blub-blub* of the tailpipe, which was at least a foot underwater. The boat drifted free of the trailer and nearly pulled Mr. Burnett in by sheer momentum, but he leaned against the rope like a stalwart deckhand. However, I was drawn spread-eagled across the bundles of gear, holding on to the rough rope for dear life. Like a rubber band, the hemp arrested and reversed the boat's motion. It glided gently up to the gravel ramp with a crunch.

The car roared away, a muddy waterfall spilling over the bumper from the open rear door. Meanwhile, I floated solo in a boat for the first time in my life. After the hoopla of splash and circumstance had passed, the boat, with its twenty-five-horsepower Evinrude outboard motor, had been successfully launched with my help. It was scary, exhilarating.

Now it was boarding time. Mr. Burnett grasped the bow. With a heave coupled with much snorting and puffing, he successfully pulled the boat a couple of more feet up the launch ramp so the men could step onto the bow without getting their feet wet. Pop slogged

"And then this fat slob..."

Pop (left), Vee Bee (right)

down the ramp and leaped aboard. He pussyfooted through all the cargo to reach his captain's bench next to the tiller of the outboard motor. An image of a bear traversing a tight rope entered my mind. His good humor was more than evident as he yelled, "Hurry up, Vee Bee! Get in the boat!"

Mr. Burnett was unable to step onto the bow. Instead, he turned around and sat down on it. I dutifully grabbed his upheld meaty left hand. "Pull Ricky," he muttered. I winced as the relentless grip of a man who had used tools his entire life clamped down on me for support.

"Put your back into it, Boy!" My father was in his element now. I struggled against Mr. Burnett's weight as he spun on his backside, thrust his short legs into the boat, and heaved himself onto the middle bench seat. "Good job," said Pop, "now get out and push us off!"

I crawled off the front of the boat and stood there, taking in the mass.

Dubious.

That's how I felt.

Planting both hands firmly on the rolled aluminum nose of the bow, I pressed into the work, gradually increasing the force until I was straining for all I was worth. The boat didn't move so much as an inch – so I tried harder. Gravel shifted under my boots. I closed my eyes in concentration. Beads of sweat rose on my forehead.

Nothing happened.

Feigning incredulity, Pop said, "What's the matter, Boy? Too heavy for you? Hey Vee Bee, it looks like we'll have to give the little fellow a hand. Get your paddle, and let's give a push."

"I don't know if that's gonna help," grumbled Mr. Burnett. He disencumbered the cypress wood paddle from under the pile of gear. Pop already had his in hand.

"What was that you said, Mr. Grumpy?"

"I might have to get out and help Ricky push. There's too much stuff in da boat! I tried to tell yah. Harrumph, heh, heh." Mr. Burnett would often puff, blow, and grumble.

"Just push, Vee Bee, but don't break my paddle! On the count of three: one, two – *push!*" They each shoved their paddles into the shallow water until they could lever against the miry bottom.

I suddenly found my leather boots filled with chilly water,

Typical load leaving the landing

blue jeans getting soaked up to the knee, and the boat sliding away. Mr. Burnett reached out and grabbed my hand. With one enormous heave, he flopped me onto the bow. The boat wallowed like a pig in mud.

"Let's go to the houseboat!" Pop gave a couple of pulls on the starter cord. The noisy outboard motor belched, coughed, and roared. We were off at last.

Since I was the smallest and lightest, weighing in at no more than sixty-five pounds, I got the front bench right on the nose of the boat. From there, I could see everything coming. The thrill lasted for all of a minute. That's how long it took to glide over to the houseboat from the launch ramp, or at least it seemed that way.

As we crossed the finger lake, the houseboat grew more prominent by the second. Pontoon-style, it sported two cylinders made of fifty-five-gallon steel drums, welded together, and filled with polystyrene foam for extra flotation. The front ends of the barrel nacelles ended in sheet metal cones. Pop told me this would allow the houseboat to glide over or around underwater obstacles more easily without knocking the pontoons from under the living quarters. Until today I hadn't understood. Gazing down into the clear water, I noticed submerged logs, stumps, and water plants sliding beneath us.

"Grab the rope!" I heard Mr. Weathers over the motor's drone, and yet another line slapped me in the face. In moments, he had us tied off alongside the houseboat. The unloading and stowing began.

Pop instructed everyone about where to put everything, but his first instruction was to me, "Get out of the way, Boy! Go stand in the corner of the porch."

"Yes, sir." Holding on to the front corner roof strut, I watched the men work. It was a relief to be out of the way of all those swinging elbows and shuffling feet. Usually, I was the gofer, going and getting whatever Pop wanted. After a while, maybe two minutes, I got kind of bored, so I began to appraise the houseboat. I noticed heavy three-quarter-inch plywood sheathing, solid two-by-four framing, windows on each side, exterior doors back and front, built to last forever. Proportionally, we are talking ten feet wide by eight feet high by twenty-eight feet long. Subtract the eight-foot front porch, and you get a rectangular living area of two hundred square feet. Talk about a tiny house.

After much furor, the boat emptied, and the houseboat filled to the eyeballs. Then came decisions on the sleeping arrangements. Four men and a boy were a stretch to fit in such a confined space comfortably. My advantage was my size. The top bunk of the triple-layer rack to the right of the entrance automatically became mine. The big boys couldn't climb up there. Opposite the bunk was a single bed. Mr. Burnett got that because he was a big boy. Pop, the biggest boy of the group, would use a portable Army cot in the center aisle. Mr. Weathers and Mr. Libner tossed a coin for the middle and lower bunks. Mr. Libner won the bottom to Mr. Weathers' chagrin.

By this time, it was mid-afternoon on Friday. Since the whole weekend's point was to test the houseboat's stability and move it out into the swamp proper, it seemed that a bit of relaxation and fishing from the porch was in order. It was the highlight of the day for me. I had never been fishing.

Out came the folding chairs, poles, bait, and beer. Pop handed me my brand-new fiberglass fishing pole sporting the world-famous Zebco 33 Spincast Reel. He dug out a fat nightcrawler from the bait cup and started showing me how to ease the worm onto my hook.

"Now look, Boy, we're gonna pinch off a chunk of this worm 'cause we're not wasteful – bait ain't cheap – and thread that bad boy right on the hook, like so." While I was getting my lesson, everyone else prepped their own gear and baited their own hooks. A tinge of impatience came over me, mainly because no one else required special attention.

"I can do it." I threaded the gooey worm onto the hook myself, cringing at the brown ichor now coating my fingers. My jeans made a good rag.

My rod-and-reel from 1968 still works great!

"Okay, Boy. Good job. Now, let me attach the bobber. What do you say, Vee Bee, about three feet deep?"

Mr. Burnett started to answer, but Mr. Weathers beat him to it. "I just got a bite, Dick. Mine's at four feet."

"Four feet it is," said Pop, adjusting the red-bottomed, white-topped bobber. "Drop it in, Boy. And don't be tugging on it. The fish won't bite if it moves too much. All you do is mash that black button on the reel, like so." He reached around me, placed my right thumb on the button, adjusted my grip on the pole, and depressed my thumb to release the line. With a soft plop, the bobber hit the water. "Okay, now let's give it a little bit of slack." He showed me how to pull a few feet of monofilament and then crank my reel's handle to stop the feed with a click. "There ya go, Boy, now just hold it steady and wait for the fish."

Happy in my own little fishing world, I felt the gentle warmth of the setting sun on my back and listened to the sounds of man-talk. Eventually, my thoughts drifted.

Like nearly everything else we owned, my rod-and-reel had come from K-Mart, another purchase in a long line of "blue light specials." I smiled to myself about how Mommy would always run through the department store to see what was marked down when the siren and blue strobe light went off. Just last week, she had flocked over with all the other women, dragging my little sister along, to a center-isle table with its winking beacon. While she was working her way into the mob to get at the specials, Pop took advantage of the distraction and pulled me over to Sporting Goods. It so happened that my rod-and-reel was on sale too for only nine-ninety-eight, not just the pantyhose at three pairs for a dollar.

Fish began to bite – but not for me. I watched as each of the men alternately would exclaim, reel in a fish, remove it from the line, drop it in the pail of water, rebait their hook, and plop their line back in for more. Impatience again crept through me. About that time, my bobber got pulled underwater. I chirped excitedly, "I've got a bite! I've got a bite!" Not really understanding how to bring in the fish with my new rod-and-reel, I simply held the rig steady. Pop was saying, "I'll be right there, Boy. Just hold whatcha got."

Something loud and buzzing zoomed by my ear, a sound that shot terror up my spine. The next thing I knew, a giant insect lit on the knuckle of my right middle finger. When I was three, I had gotten myself into a nest of ground hornets in our front yard. It meant a trip to the emergency room for an epinephrine shot, as I had been covered in stings from head to toe – pain that I could never forget. I instantly recognized the sound and the shape of that inch-long black wasp.

Pop said, "Don't move, Boy. He won't sting unless you scare him!"

Scare him? What about me? I held steady, eyes fastened on that nasty bug, my body locked ridged in fear. Just then, the fish that I had hooked decided to fight back. The pole, and hence, my hand, jerked. With perfect clarity, I saw the wasp inject his stinger into my knuckle, and searing pain shot all the way to my elbow.

From the way the men turned their heads to give me privacy, I'm sure I was blubbering. Pop swatted the wasp away and handed off my pole to Mr. Libner. Jealously I watched through smeared eyeglasses as he reeled in my first catch – a pan-sized sunfish bream with yellowish stripes, blue gills, and a golden throat. He then removed the hook from the bream's mouth and dropped it in the pail with all the others. It was the ultimate letdown.

I noticed that Mr. Weathers got busy crushing the tobacco out of some of his cigarettes into his palm. He then stuck the dried brown leaves into his mouth and started chewing. In short order, he spat a blob of runny tobacco back into his palm. It seemed like a waste of cigarettes to me.

Pop said, "Gimme your hand, Son." He used his fingernails to extract the black stinger from my knuckle, or so I assumed. "It's okay now. When the bug stings you, it rips out his guts." He then dug a

Public domain image by Alejandro Santillana. Produced as part of the "Insects Unlocked" project. The University of Texas at Austin.

The Great Black Wasp (*Sphex pensylvanicus*) is found all over the Continental United States. They sting in defense of their nest. Unlike bees, their stingers are not barbed, so their abdomens do not rip out when they attack. Therefore, they can sting continuously while injecting venom containing five percent acetylcholine, a toxic chemical extremely painful to humans.

white handkerchief out of his back pocket and held it forth for Mr. Weathers to deposit the messy wad of tobacco. To my horror, Pop slapped that spit-laden blob onto my knuckle and trussed up my finger. "Now, just hold this tobacco on the sting for a while, and the pain will go away. Feel better?"

Although the pain had not begun to subside, I had to admit that the idea of the wasp dying violently did, at some level, satisfy my sense of justice. It was not until years later that I learned wasps really do not die after stinging. That evening I was able to remove the sloppy tobacco poultice from my finger. The knuckle did indeed feel much better. I could grasp my fork, which made all the difference for filling my continually growling belly.

Mr. Burnett was an excellent cook, a skill he had learned in the National Guard. Given salt, pepper, flour, cornmeal, eggs, and scalding vegetable oil, he could make the most excellent fried fish on the planet. As for proper nutrition, sure, you can always overindulge in fried foods, but if you're a health fanatic, you're missing out on one of life's greatest pleasures. Nothing beats the satisfaction of eating the tender white meat of freshly caught, battered, and fried bream.

I contemplated my swollen knuckle, which would eventually heal, as I polished off a dozen of those Santee delicacies. It wasn't so bad, getting stung again. Sure, it was embarrassing to have cried in front of the men – a fleeting instance in the Grand Scheme – and something they had probably done at one time or another. After dinner, packed to the brim with bream, I crawled up in my top bunk and felt quite cozy hunkered down in my K-mart Brand navy blue sleeping bag. As my eyes closed for the night, I realized that sometimes a little pain must be endured as part of life. It makes us even more appreciative of the pleasures that come our way.

"Man must go back to nature for information."
~ Thomas Paine

Dead Forest

"Stay up there outta the way, Boy." Pop got busy getting the others busy. The weather had held overnight, so the sun was shining, and things were so far, so good on the day of the Big Move.

Everything seemed big to me, as it was all part of the first-time experience. I could see the Big Water out the front door of the houseboat, after having eaten a Big Breakfast from a Big Plate covered with Big Ribbons of Bacon heaped with Big Spoons full of scrambled eggs cooked in the drippings.

Following instructions, I laid in my bunk studying the grain and knots of the gray plywood ceiling, thinking how nice it must be to be Big, as in fully grown. People wouldn't order you to do this and that and tell you what you can and can't do all the time. Peripherally, I saw capped heads hustling around – working. I decided to keep my mouth shut.

Raw materials from the Big Breakfast were stowed back in the coolers for tomorrow morning. The beds got straightened. Pop's cot got folded away. Trash got stuffed in a Big Garbage Bag. The Big Potty Sack was carefully tied off, triple-bagged, and placed back inside the white plastic pail sporting a toilet lid in the corner...uuuugh. Pop had warned everyone right up front, but especially me, not to bust the potty sack. Thankfully, I hadn't had to use that yet and was determined to hold it till I got home. Besides, I was unsure why everyone else kept making jokes about praying to Ralph, the porcelain god. There wasn't any porcelain aboard, and I wouldn't pray to it if there was. It must have something to do with the makeshift toilet.

Pop ran an orderly outfit. It made me feel better as I listened to him doling out instructions to everyone else while I stayed put, not that he was bossy, mind you. The guys seemed to accept that he knew what to do, how to do it, and when to get it done. And he was Bigger than anyone else.

I had gotten enough attention earlier as I drank from a glass bottle of whole milk. The men apparently didn't like milk, or maybe I put them in mind of something I had discovered only a week ago. The milkman had left a note on the side door that said it was his last delivery. He was going out of business. Apparently, the grocery store offered lower prices than he could match to get it for yourself off the shelves in newfangled wax paper cartons. Mommy had not been happy. Maybe it was because it was only another thing for her to have to remember to do.

Whiffs of skillet-cooked, smoky slabs of bacon drifted up to me as the trash bag was tied off. My mouth watered, and my stomach rumbled – again. We had only just finished eating, so I knew better than to tell Pop I was still hungry. Everyone would want to know where such a small boy could put all that I ate. Now I wished once more to be an adult. Pop always told me to be careful what I wished for.

"You must have a hollow leg," Mr. Libner had said over breakfast. "We'll have to keep it filled so you'll build up your strength for my karate class at the YMCA. I'll bet you can hardly wait for summer vacation so we can get started. Did you know that my hands are registered as lethal weapons?" He held them out for all to see.

"No, sir, I didn't." He was right about summer vacation, but I wasn't so sure about karate. I didn't know what that was.

"Yeah, the Army sent me to Nam to fight the Vietcong, and I came back a black belt. They shipped me over right out of high school, and that was years ago! I can't believe we're still there fighting. If the politicians would get out of the military's way, we'd cream them."

While I knew that Vietnam was the war we were currently fighting overseas, mainly because it was on CBS Evening News at seven o'clock with Walter Cronkite every night, I still didn't understand what it meant to be a black belt. Would I be able to fight bad guys? Mother always told me to never, ever hit anyone, not ever, but especially not my little sister, Melanie. It didn't matter how

**Lt. Colonel Paul H. Bjorkman, Retired
Air Force Navigator and Father-In-Law**

"The Vietnam War was fought between the communist North Vietnamese and the U.S.-supported South Vietnamese. The communists wanted to unify the whole country, but the U.S. fought alongside the South Vietnamese to keep them free. The whole war lasted from 1955 to 1975 and only ended when the U.S. withdrew. Within two years, the Vietcong (North Vietnamese) imposed communism on the southern populace. As the war continued into the Sixties, American news media began to downplay our involvement. Public opinion, driven by the youth of America, turned against the war. Thus, the Hippies were born. In their bell-bottomed blue jeans worn low on the hip, long hair, and tie-dyed shirts sporting the upside-down broken cross in a circle – the Peace Symbol – they stormed across America rioting and protesting in what is now called the Peace Movement. The tide of public opinion rose to such a negative height that our military veterans were reviled as warmongers and spat upon when they were recalled from battle. They returned home disgraced, neither having won the war nor appreciated for doing their duty as American soldiers."

much of my stuff she broke. On the other hand, my dad had told me on numerous occasions not to throw the first punch, but if someone hit me, hit them back harder and make sure I finished the fight. I didn't want to fight anybody.

Mr. Libner continued, "Just look at these hands, mind you. I spent months sticking them in and out of a bowl of ground glass to toughen them up with callouses. Now I can break boards all day without tearing the skin or getting a bruise. Feel them, Ricky."

"Libner, stop scaring the boy!" Pop was smiling when he said it. "Your mouth runs on like a meandering creek." Mr. Libner held up a peace sign but made no further comment.

I reached out and felt the leathery skin just to prove I wasn't afraid. Looking back on it, that might be why Pop had said what he did. He was first-rate about teaching without letting on that he was. As far as Mr. Libner goes, he was a wiry sort of guy with straight brown hair, shoulder-length. His radiant blue eyes were always animated like his mouth. And he was the only one I knew with

Author's Son Douglas Meehan
I played Cowboys and Indians when I was a child. The term Native American only started showing up in the 1990s. My son looks just like me, except I had a cap gun and holster on my hip that made noise and smoke.

one-fourth Cherokee Indian blood in him. He was *cool*, a new term I had learned at Jessie Boyd Elementary School for anything mind-blowing. Before that, everything was groovy, man – everything except double-knit polyester pants. Wearing that new synthetic cloth was like donning a plastic bag. Moisture could not escape, and it was anything but cool. However, the wild color patterns woven into much of the fabrics of that time were groovy, man.

"Okay, boys, it's time to get to the boats," Pop said. "Ricky, up in your bunk till I call you back down." Wow. Pop called me by my name. That meant things must be getting serious. I scrambled up and out of the way again.

Mr. Weathers, blonde handlebar mustache quivering, piped up, "Which boat is Don going in, Dick?"

"Look, Weathers, you just get in your little boat, and Vee Bee'll get in my little boat, and Don will take his pick of whoever's willing to listen to him talk all day."

Mr. Weathers said, "Vernon. Let's draw straws. Short straw gets Don." He freed a golden-yellow pack of cigarettes from the upturned cuff of his tee-shirt, expertly popped one out, then tossed the carton to the table so I could admire the cool picture of a camel standing in front of a pyramid. With a great flourish, he broke the cigarette in two and stuck the pieces in his fist. Now both butts appeared the same length.

"Awww…dammit! I'm not that bad!" blustered Mr. Libner.

"Remember what I told you before we came down, Libner! Profanity is a no-no." Pop glanced slyly in my direction. "His momma would have a nut if Mr. Walking Tape Recorder up there was to repeat any of it. And Boy, remember what I told you – what happens down at Santee stays down at Santee. Got it?" I kept my mouth shut.

"Oh yeah, sorry. I just meant that –" began Mr. Libner.

Vernon interrupted, "Hush, Donny. We're busy." He reached out and promptly selected the short straw. "Awwwww! Go git in da boat! Humph, humph." And in a mumble, "Gotta listen to that mouth all day…gonna be a long one… can't believe my luck."

"Well, don't make it sound like I'm a burden or something," said Mr. Libner. "Just because I try to be sociable. Here I was, gonna offer y'all free karate lessons so y'all can protect yourselves, and this is what I get for it."

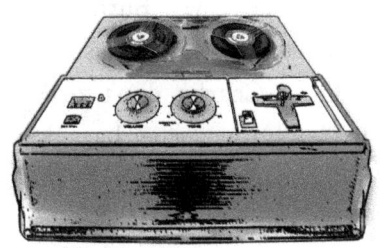

Reel-to-Reel Tape Recorder
Tape recorders for personal use were an amazing novelty back in the 1960s. Like their professional relatives, the reel-to-reel studio versions with nearly one-foot-diameter reels of thin magnetic tape, these portable models, if you can call an eighteen-inch-square by the eight-inch-high metal box "portable," were used for recording special sounds like my baby noises.

"Now, Libner, don't go getting your panties in a wad. We'll take your little self-defense class when we get back. For now, just get in the boat and try not to drive poor little Vee Bee insane. Me and Rick have got to ride back home with him tomorrow. He's already touchy enough."

Mr. Libner was beginning to explain the details on how he came to be part Injun on his mother's side as he and Mr. Burnett gathered up equipment to take with them. Colorful beer cans figured prominently, sporting labels like Pabst Blue Ribbon, Falstaff, and Old Milwaukee. These cans were not pop-top but flat-top. Mr. Libner brought out a brand-new handheld transistor radio from his duffle bag and turned it on to a bunch of static. Thumbing the tuning dial, he bopped out the door to the Beatles singing *Twist and Shout*.

Hung-dog, Mr. Burnett trailed him out the door muttering, "He'd better turn that noise down, or I'll...harrumph."

"Okay, Charlie, don't forget your sack of beer." Pop tossed him a loaded brown paper bag. "Make sure to tie off that tow rope the way I showed you. We don't want to damage anything. Whatever you do, don't run over Vee Bee and Libner."

"See you in a bit, Dick." Mr. Weathers fitted a cigarette to his lips and stalked out to his flat-bottomed rental boat. It only had a ten-horse motor, which sounded like a couple of bumblebees' wings when it got started. Still, Pop was sure it would have gracious power for helping tow the houseboat to its new home.

"Come on down now," said Pop.

I climbed from my top bunk, carefully placing my feet on the bunk below, and likewise for the one below that. My stomach rumbled again. "How long will it be before they all come back for lunch, Pop?"

"It'll be hours yet. The day's just getting started, Boy." The tone of his voice told me that he might be playing his mind-reading game again. He knew I was hungry.

"I need to go to the bathroom," I said.

"Number One or Number Two?"

"Number One."

"So, open the back door and hang it off the side. Just like you did last night."

I plodded over to the door, threw it open, thinking that this was yet another deal where the Big People got their jollies at my expense. Ever try taking a pee while others are watching and jeering? The urge was too bad now to worry about decorum, however. I did a one-handed operation while bracing myself with the other hand firmly gripping the door frame. The boat began to rock, which made everything more difficult. Noticing that there were no waves,

I looked over my shoulder to see Pop sidling back and forth in the aisle, making the boat sway.

Pop smirked, "Don't piss into the wind, Boy!" Just then, a gust blew my little yellow stream all over my hands and down part of my pants leg.

"Haahhaahhaaaa!"

Lesson learned. Don't pee when the Big Boys are looking.

I got done and went over to the full-sized stainless-steel sink to wash my hands. Pop had rigged a lift-handle steel drum pump that would bring lake water into the sink. He said not to drink it but to wash hands in it. I dropped the drain plug in place and drew the handle up and down to get the water going. While I lathered with the dirty bar soap and rinsed my hands in the lake water, I had to admit that the sink setup was smart. I felt like Daniel Boone, blazing trails into unknown and exciting territories.

Sufficiently restored, I turned to ask, "Where does the dirty water go?"

"Into the swamp, Boy."

"Won't that hurt the fish?"

"Fish eat a lot worse than anything we put in the swamp. Besides, soap will rot to become fertilizer. That means bigger fish." He was a chemist by profession, after all.

"Oh." I tried to imagine what fish ate that could be worse.

"Looks like we'll be seeing Vee Bee and Libner again fairly shortly." I wondered what he meant. They were out fiddling around, tying ropes and stuff to the front of the houseboat. "They forgot something important." Pop held up a church key and snickered, "Can't open the beer without it. Hey, I read in the paper the other day that we will have another rocket launch in October – Apollo 7. You thirsty? Let's finish up this Tang. Maybe you'd like another doughnut too." Without waiting for my answer, he poured up two paper cups and handed one to me, opened the powdered donuts, and shoved the bag my way.

I would never turn down the heavily orange-flavored, sweet-and-sour drink used by the astronauts, nor a fat donut! We didn't get donuts at home except on infrequent occasions. They were considered an unnecessary household expense. On the other hand, Tang was far cheaper and less trouble than squeezing the juice out of real oranges. One serving contained one hundred percent of the recommended daily allowance of vitamin C required for a growing boy. Mommy made it all the time. She called it "economical."

Pop knew how I loved to watch the rocket launches on television. They were black-and-white wonders to behold – lots of smoke, light, and fury – science fiction becoming fact. Visions of

Church Key
The nickname of the common can and bottle opener required to open drinks. Pop tops, push tops, and plastic screw-lid bottles had not yet arrived on the scene. A church key manually punched a triangular hole in the top edge of the can or levered off the cap on a bottle. In the case of a can, you would make a big punch on one side and a little punch opposite, so air could enter as the liquid was removed. Otherwise, it was hard to get the liquid to pour without slopping it all over oneself.

Duck Tale 33

myself in a spacesuit were crushed when a sudden flurry of outdoor activity drew our attention.

"You broke my radio!" It was Mr. Libner yelling.

"Harrumph! I did not. Lookie here – it says, 'Made in Japan.' You shoulda known better 'n to buy something made in Japan. Ain't nothin' but garbage! Everybody knows that."

Pop lumbered out to the porch. "Boys, boys. Quit playing with your toys, and let's go. We've got a long day ahead. Libner, have you tied off the tow rope properly?" Mr. Libner gave a thumbs-up. "Yo, Charlie. You ready?"

"Good to go, Dick."

"Alright. No screwing around! I don't want anybody getting hurt or a boat torn up because you got too wild and weren't paying attention. Charlie, put that beer down. It's too early in the day for that! How'd you get it open anyway? I've got the church key."

"Just wetting my whistle," said Mr. Weathers, grinning. "Knives work wonders too." He did put the beer down, though – until Pop looked the other way.

My Hitachi Cassette Tape Deck
Back in 1968, if it said "Made in Japan" on the label, you could guarantee it would not last very long. Today, Japanese goods are some of the finest in the world. My Hitachi tape deck is a great example. I've had it since 1981 and it still works great!

Pop knelt to check the heavy ropes from each boat that were now tethered to the tow ring. The large metal eye bolt had been mounted to the front of the porch's framework, centered between the pontoons. "Looks good, Boys. Libner, did you untie us from the trees?"

"You're free, Dick."

"Okay. Y'all, take it easy! Rev'em up, and let's go!" Pop waved his arms and pointed. I supposed it was in the general direction we were headed.

Mr. Burnett and Mr. Weathers both pulled their motors to life. Each boat began to slide away from the houseboat, stretching the ropes until they became taut. And…WHAM! The two boats collided as the tension on the ropes transferred energy toward the center.

"I told you to watch out!" Pop hollered. "Aim the boats away from each other so they don't hit again!"

No one got hurt. The boats didn't get damaged. Once the pilots angled off to the left and right, everything began to work out. Pop and I grabbed folding metal chairs and sat down on the porch to watch the show.

Mr. Burnett and Mr. Weathers kept their eyes on each other. They waved and pointed to communicate such things as adjusting angle and speed as necessary. We could hear Mr. Libner yapping over the whine of the engines. The houseboat was towed in a gentle arc toward the main river channel. As the three boats entered the river, everything became simpler. The current was pushing us downstream in the direction we needed to go. The boats cavitated as they increased power but stabilized as speeds were matched. Everything was going smoothly, for now.

Pop and I had a great view off the front porch in the sunshine glinting off the black water. A warm breeze flowed through the open doors, making things comfortable and lazy. Other boats would pass by now and again, with fellow boaters waving and admiring our production. After a while, we eventually came to a tributary off to the left that we had to take. Motors whined about making the turn. The houseboat swung around, leaning top heavily with the change in course until the current grabbed the pontoons and started working against us. Mr. Weathers' little rental boat became a liability as the small motor was no match for the strain. Pop's boat took up the slack. At least the water flow would be pushing us again once we entered the tributary.

There was only enough space for one boat in the middle once we made it into the narrow creek. Some hasty adjustments had to be made. Pop yelled for Mr. Weathers to cut his motor, then untied his boat, and motioned him to swing around behind the houseboat to become a push engine against the framework. Mr. Burnett continued to tug straight down the center of the creek.

For a moment, it looked like everything was going to work out fine. Then, the pontoons dragged bottom, halting our forward momentum. Mr. Weathers' boat tried to climb up through the backdoor. I had never heard some of the strange words that began to issue from my father's mouth as he jumped from his seat to rush to

Cut to the Dead Forest
Years later I took my young family through this creek to show them the Dead Forest when we surprised a large alligator sunning itself on the muddy bank. The reptile tried to run over us in its haste to get away. It was the only time I ever saw an alligator at Santee although I heard them moaning at night many times.

the back. They were probably part of that rule, "What happens at Santee, stays at Santee."

"Weathers," Pop yelled, "Put it in reverse!" He strained against the bow of Mr. Weathers' boat, attempting to lift the hull from the threshold, back and arm muscles bulging with the effort. Pop told me once about how he played a lot of football in high school and college. I wondered if I would ever grow to be that strong. The boat pulled away. Pop made a slash sign across his throat so Mr. Weathers would cut his engine. Pop came back to the porch and did the same at Mr. Burnett. "Huddle up, Boys. We've got to make a new plan."

Well, the new idea included what I would call worrying the houseboat through the channel and out into the vast expanse of the dead cypress forest ahead. First, everything that wasn't nailed down had to be reloaded into the boats to lighten the houseboat in hopes that it would float. Everyone got wet except me. I was told to stay out of the way again. Mr. Burnett's motor spewed muddy water everywhere. Pop and Mr. Libner had to get in the creek to push against the pontoons while keeping Mr. Weathers' boat trained against the houseboat's transom so it wouldn't climb up in the back-door again. They struggled through a mucky mess, becoming coated in black mud. By midafternoon, the houseboat drifted free of the confining creek.

After a break, the mudpuppies sat on the porch and had me pour buckets of Santee water over them to remove all the muck. Once satisfied everyone was clean enough, Pop suggested they change to dry clothes, get snacks of pickled eggs and hot sausages, and more than a few beers. Thus fortified, the Big Boys were ready for the final stretch. I observed the activity while munching a Baby Ruth candy bar. Peanuts, chocolate, and gooey caramel – yum. Life couldn't get much better than this.

The gear was stowed back in the houseboat. The tugboats were back in front with ropes tied. Motors wound up. We were underway again.

By four o'clock, the final location was reached. The houseboat was temporarily tied off with ropes between two colossal dead cypress trees. The men broke out half-inch galvanized steel cabling and clamps and stretched the cables to replace the ropes. The heavy clamps ensured that the cables could not come loose from either the trees or the houseboat. We were moored.

As the whitish sun sank between heavy black clouds and water on the horizon, I took in the surrounding forest. Dead cypress trees – tall and weathered to gray – rose eerily from the watery expanse. It reminded me of an army of pale ghosts watching the sunset in silence. Shivers slinked up my spine.

There was not much banter that night. The men were, in my father's words, dead-dog-tired. Mr. Burnett still cooked up a storm of food as the darkness grew. Several hamburgers, charbroiled to perfection over a large charcoal grill on the porch, smothered in all the fixings, but most especially catsup, filled my belly comfortably. A few more beers later, and the men had had enough for one day. We all turned in.

About the time my eyes finally closed despite all the snoring, a storm broke. The wind screamed through the Dead Forest, whipping up sizable waves. The houseboat started tossing around like the *S. S. Minnow* on the CBS television sitcom *Gilligan's Island*. In terror, I clung to the foam mattress to prevent myself from falling out of the bunk.

The houseboat seemed to rock and roll endlessly. It slammed back and forth between its new mooring cables until I was sure it would be ripped apart. The boats crashed against us, threatening to bash holes in the plywood sheathing. Sometimes water washed under the front door and sloshed against the backdoor, while other times, the opposite happened. Pop was telling everybody it was going to be okay, just to stay in our bunks. The only illumination came from the monstrous lightning strikes; the immediate thunder rattled my teeth from its concussion. Inside that small wooden box, we were helpless.

When the tempest finally broke, Pop managed to light a couple of large candles to view the situation. The floor was awash. Pots and pans were strewn everywhere, along with cups, plates, utensils, and anything else that wasn't nailed down. I could tell that all the Big Boys were relieved the storm was over. So was I.

Pop found his two-cell flashlight, squished his way in sock feet to the front door, threw it open. The beam played over one of the boats. From my high angle, I could see water sloshing around at the bottom of it.

Pop must have been satisfied that everything was okay. He came back in to tell us, "That was a helluva storm – but we're alive – and better yet, our boats are still out there, so we don't have to swim. All we've got to do is a little bailing in the morning. The stars are out, the moon is bright. Everything is right with the world. Let's get some sleep!"

"A man must be both stupid and uncharitable who believes there is no virtue or truth but on his own side."
~ Joseph Addison

Shades of Gray

Pop discovered Pack's Landing on Lake Marion's upper side in his quest to get to the Happy Hunting Grounds as quickly as possible. Pack's was closer than going through Lone Star and Cameron to Low Falls Landing. There was no fast way to go from

Spartanburg to Santee until they built the I-26 connector to Charleston in the early '80s. The top of the lake around Rimini was a wilderness at the time.

Unfortunately, Pop hadn't accounted for the extra two miles over water from the new landing to the houseboat. Eventually, this would lead to the Big Move, but for now, it took over an hour by boat from the launch. As we traveled, my mind imagined crawling southwest along the Seaboard Coast Line creosote railroad trestle to the river. From there, we would turn downriver to the creek. Then we would head north across shallow open water to the Dead Forest. The boat would encounter sandbars and stumps in the pitch dark. Just thinking on it was harrowing, especially since I would be lighting the way with only a wane beam from a D-Cell flashlight. Nowadays, this is no big deal as the newer boats have bright LED headlamps, and their motors can take the pounding from the underwater stumps. It was frightening just to think about it as we traveled.

"Don't let me forget that we gotta stop for bait at the Brass Ankle Store," Pop was saying to Mr. Burnett. "Some of that smoked fish they have in that big ole wooden barrel ought to do the trick. It smells high enough."

"Dem black folks sure know how to make de bait, er, ah, harrumph, don't dey, Dick?"

"Sure do, Vee Bee. The smell alone must drive those catfish crazy. Remember the last time when we caught that thirty-pound monster?"

"Yeah, heh, heh. Had to shoot it in the head with my pistol before we could skin it. It opened my palm to the bone with its dang fin. Hurt like a son-of-a-b-b-b-buh." Mr. Burnett petered out on whatever he was planning to say and looked in the rearview mirror at me.

"Why is it called the Brass Ankle Store?" I yelled over the rub-

Duck Tale

Author kayaking a half-mile from the Seaboard Coast Line railroad trestle in broad daylight with excellent weather and no fog in Pack's Flats.
Photo courtesy of Michael Free, 2018.

rub-rub-rub of the mud grip tires on the rough country road from my middle bench seat in Pop's new vehicle. The day he brought the orange-and-white Toyota Land Cruiser FJ55 home, he dubbed it the Toy.

Pop said, "Because the woman who runs the place is of mixed race, meaning she had one black parent and one that was white. Brass is the color of her skin. You'll get to see her shortly."

Since I had met only one black person in my whole life to this point, I got nervous. Just last week, I had been waiting for my mother to pick me up from my after-school swimming lessons at the Spartanburg YMCA, and a black boy had come in the front entrance. I was playing bumper pool by myself; no one else was around. He was about my age – nine or ten perhaps. He asked if he could play pool with me. I said, "Sure." He grabbed a cue.

For the next fifteen or so minutes, we eyed each other over the round green table as we took our shots, not saying a word. I noticed the hair on the other boy's head was quite nappy and so black that the overhead lighting had glistened from it as if reflected by a thousand tiny mirrors. His brown eyes were piercing, most likely because the whites showed up starkly against his even darker skin. Just then, the manager came out of the glass-enclosed main office and headed straight to our pool table.

"What are you doing, boy? This is a whites-only establishment. You know you're not allowed here. Come with me."

"Yes, sir." My playmate's eyes met mine as he gently laid the cue across the table. They were reddened, watery, and contained a haunted look – humiliation. I watched the manager escort the black boy to the exit. A sense of terrible shame washed over me for reasons I had not yet tried to understand.

Now, as I watched the passing pine forests out the window of the Toy, I shuddered to think how it would feel to enter a non-white business and to meet a Brass Ankle. Would we be welcome in her store?

The road had narrowed to become nearly a pig path, or so it seemed. We bounced over a railroad track, jostling my insides most uncomfortably. I gripped the edge of the tan vinyl-covered bench seat as best I could to keep from smacking my head on the ceiling.

None of us were wearing seatbelts. This was the first automobile Pop had that offered those safety devices. Mine was stuffed down on either side of me between the seat cushions. I pushed my hands down there and grabbed them for support.

"Are we there yet?" I asked the age-old question of every child stuck in the back of a moving vehicle for hours at a time. There was nothing to do but look out the window at the passing scenery.

"Yeah, we are, Boy! You've been awfully quiet back there. Are you gittin' hungry?" I could see Pop eyeing me in the rearview mirror and felt the ribbing coming on.

Mr. Burnett added his two cents worth with an empathetic "Me too, Dick. Mebbe they still got some of them hot pickled pig's feet an' pig knuckles. Harrumph, meh, heh, heh."

"Boy, we might find you a goodie at the Brass Ankle, but you'll have to come in with us to pick it out. I kinda doubt you can handle pig's feet. Maybe they've got some of those great big sour dill pickles. That'll hold you for a while till we get to the houseboat."

The store turned out to be a low, dingy, concrete block building with a gas pump out front. Although we didn't need a fill-up, there was nowhere else to park hauling a boat and trailer except between the road and the pump, so Pop pulled up next to it.

"We aren't going to be but a minute," he said. "Vee Bee, be careful hopping out in the middle of the road. Boy, don't bang the door against the pump. Let's go."

As my leather boots hit the gravel, the troubled eyes of the black boy I had met at the Y loomed up in my brain. Worms of dread squirmed in my belly, but I wasn't about to let the men know how awkward I was feeling.

"Whatcha waiting for, Boy, come on in." Pop and Mr. Burnett were already stumping through the open screen door. I noticed the door had been propped with what looked like a small iron pedestal with a flattened shoe on the top. I took a big breath and crossed the threshold.

The inside was murky. There was a smoldering potbelly stove in the back-left corner. Next to it, on rickety chairs around a small table covered in playing cards, sat five dark people, two women and three men. All of them held cigarettes; the air was stale with smoke. The women wore garish tight dresses. Their ankles sported rings upon rings of shiny bracelets my mother would describe as old gold in color. Their arms were draped over the men's shoulders, showing more cleavage than I had ever seen. All were staring at me as if I had interrupted an important meeting.

Shoeshine Footrest

At the time I didn't know that the strange device was a shoeshine footrest used in the airports or train hubs of big cities like New York. People would simply walk up, take a seat that was usually provided, and prop a foot on the pedestal. A black man, referred to as a shoeshine boy, would whip out a soft cloth, a little shoe polish, and start buffing. The final touch for a mirror finish was for the shoeshine boy to spit on the toe and buff a few more seconds vigorously. Saliva is acidic and would react with the waxy polish. Once done, a person could see oneself in the shine; thus, the term *spit shine* was born. The cost was 10 cents a pair or 5 cents a shoe in the early 1960s. Today that price is ten bucks a pair and the shoeshine *technician* doesn't like to polish only one shoe.

Tearing my eyes away, I noticed the shelf to my left was sparsely covered in canned foods and candy. To my right was a large wooden barrel with a round wooden lid. A handwritten cardboard sign was nailed to the front of the barrel that said, "Smoked Fish." It didn't say what type. Behind a short counter stood a rather strapping, brass-colored woman. She wore an autumn plaid dress and was puffing on a thick cigar that had burned nearly down to the nub. A few shelves behind her contained cigarettes, lighter fluid, and flints. Laying on the slat board counter were what looked like hunting knives. Pop and Mr. Burnett were both fingering them for sharpness and talking to the strange woman. I got a distinct impression that we were not wanted here, but neither my father nor Mr. Burnett noticed. Instead, they began to haggle with the woman over the price of the knives.

She spoke in a guttural tone, which I learned later came from having smoked too much. "I ain't takin no less than twenty dollars apiece."

"Harrumph. Come on, Dick. That's way too much."

"Now, Vee Bee. Just hold your horses. Bessy here's just mulling it over. She knows we ain't gonna pay that much."

"You will if you want dem knives," Bessy growled. She started picking something from under one of her long, red-painted fingernails with a penknife of her own. "Dem knives was made by my late husband. It took him a month o' Sundays to finish'em. You want'em, you pay. Twenty dollars."

Pop got a sly look on his face. "What if we buy some other stuff, like say, some of that smoked fish in that barrel over yonder. Would you come off the price then?"

Bessy folded her penknife and stuffed it away in a tightly stretched pocket over one of her ample breasts. Her biceps swelled like some of the men I had seen at the YMCA when she planted her fists on her broad hips. "I done told yah – NO! Now, if you 'uns ain't gonna pay, get on outta here!"

There was a scraping of chairs from the corner.

Mr. Burnett tugged at Pop's sleeve. "Let's git da fish and go, Dick." They both laid the knives back on the counter.

"Rick," said Pop to me, "Pull about six of them fish outta the barrel. Bessy, you got a bag we can put them in?"

"Naw." She reached under her counter and drew out a brown cardboard tray, the kind canned goods come packed on. "Just throw'em here. That'll be six dollars."

"Six dollars!" Pop puffed up to his full imposing height.

Bessy waggled her head side-to-side as she spoke, "That's what I said!"

I lifted the lid and started pulling long ebony fish from the barrel by their tails and laying them up in the tray. They were stiff and smelled like smoked pork barbeque. My belly rumbled.

"How about throwing in a Baby Ruth for the young man?" My dad eyed Bessy with one thick brow raised expectantly.

Bessy squinted over my way as if she was appraising a piece of costume jewelry. A candy bar had magically appeared on top of the pile of fish.

Pop pulled out a five, and Mr. Burnett passed over a single bill. I noticed the corner group was still awfully quiet. "Come on, Boy." He handed me the Baby Ruth, balanced the tray of fish in one hand, and steered me out the door with the other. Mr. Burnett was leading the way. As if Bessy had willed it to close, the wood-framed screen door slammed of itself the moment we exited the building. The strange iron prop had fallen off the step. From the furtive glances between the two men, I could tell that they were as glad as me to have escaped with our scalps. My skin was crawling with the distinct feeling that we were indeed not welcome in that store. I wondered if the black boy at the *Y* had felt this way as he was shone the exit.

It was growing dark when we pulled into Pack's Landing. While the men started the usual flurry of boat loading and launching activity, I finished my candy bar, mainly staying out of the way so I wouldn't get run over. The discomfort I had felt at the Brass Ankle

Store could not compete with the uneasiness now welling up inside me over traveling through the swamp at night.

"Git in the yacht, Boy! We're heading to the houseboat!" Yacht? I found this term much easier to understand, so I stepped from the rickety old pier into my spot on the very front bench at the bow. My new canvas hunting hat slipped down over my eyes and ears, too big now, but I knew I'd grow into it eventually. I pushed it back up so I could see, but the warmth around the tops of my ears was welcome.

On this occasion, it was a mild spring weekend. Pop had told me to pack warmly and wear my clothes in peel-able layers. The nighttime low would be about forty-five, and the daytime high about seventy-two. I had been camping a few times now, so I knew how to pack my own bags and keep up with my gear. Mommy had labeled most of my stuff with my name, even my socks and underwear. I buttoned my jacket as we worked our way out of the landing. The darkness swallowed us as surely as the whale had Jonah.

The main thing about leaving Pack's is that the side current and water level vary depending upon recent rainfall. Essentially, Pack's Flats results from the confluence of the Congaree and Wateree rivers a few miles north. If rain has been heavy, the excess water will spill over the Santee Cooper dam, some miles to the southeast, at the rate of eighteen million gallons per minute. This evening the current was weak because there had been no recent rain. When the water is slow, the water level is low, making some stumps visible. I was alert, scanning ahead of us in the encroaching darkness for shadows of stumps in the water.

Our boat was slam full of gear as usual as we left the landing – guns, ammo, fishing poles, bait, drinks, food, duffle bags of clothes, boots, sneakers, and much more. Don't forget the combined weight of the passengers, about five hundred pounds. All total, we were probably pushing half a ton in a boat made of aircraft aluminum.

Filled with worry, I sat rigid on my boat cushion, gripping a four-cell metal flashlight. It was not turned on, merely ready in case needed. Since D-cell batteries didn't last very long, Pop had warned me not to play with the light until he told me to turn it on. He said navigating the watercourses by moonlight would save the batteries. Tonight, only the feeble running lights required by law made any dent in our surroundings, as the moon was barely breaking through a thin cloud layer. My mind conjured many hazards in the moist darkness, but my prior experience with striking stumps was in the forefront. While the boat was well constructed, that didn't mean it was indestructible. Cypress stumps were hardy and unforgiving. You could barely chip one with an ax. Just then, the boat lurched upward on the port side to the tune of wham, bam, blam, whap! SCREEEEECH!

A cooler slammed into my legs, and I nearly rolled into the water. If Mr. Burnett hadn't grabbed the back of my collar, I would have. Pop gunned the engine. After an eternity, the transom slipped over the stump, and the boat righted itself. Unfortunately, the foot of the motor hit the stump next. Outboard motors were not on hydraulic lifts, nor were they necessarily held in a locked-down position. The Evinrude bucked up and pivoted into Pop's lap with a loud whing-ding-ding-ding-DING as the prop left the water. He cut the throttle and pushed the motor back down.

"Did we lose anybody?"

"A heh, heh, heh. Ricky almost went in duh drink." Mr. Burnett was still holding my collar. His voice had a nervous tinge. "I don't think we lost anything."

"Hey Boy, maybe you'd better turn on the light!" Pop jerked the motor back to life, and we were off again. "Onward!"

Gratefully, I pushed the slider switch on the flashlight and allowed the beam to play out in front of the boat. It really wasn't much better than using a jug of fireflies like a lantern, but I supposed it was better than nothing.

Having no further hiccups except for a few tips and bumps, we finally arrived at the houseboat. It loomed eerily out of the thin layer of fog now drifting through the Dead Forest but was nevertheless a welcome sight. Or should I say that an irrational urge to leap to the porch and prostrate myself flowed through me?

"Vee Bee," began Pop, "we have got to figure a better way. This whole deal just takes too long. Here it is ten o'clock already, and we haven't eaten yet."

"Ah know, ah know. Mumph, heh, heh. Maybe that's what we gotta do tomorrow. I sure can't see us trying to do dis during duck season. We wouldn't get no sleep."

That was the last time I recall traveling the long route to the houseboat. During that weekend, we scouted out a new mooring, one protected from prying eyes and lousy weather, a heavenly location in the thick of a duck swamp. By the time we left for home, I was an old hand at spotting stumps and going against the flow when the boat tilted unexpectedly.

I sat on the porch, watching the sun drop below the treetops and thinking how Santee was such a respite from the doldrums of everyday life. Being outdoors drove racial concerns, among other serious things, out of my head. Just then, the mouthwatering aroma of Vernon's salt-and-pepper fried catfish drifted past, making me wonder when dinner would be ready. Obviously, the needs of the stomach outweighed heavy thoughts.

A few weeks later was the Big Move Part Deux. To pull it off, Pop enlisted three buddies, three boats, and me. As more of a casual observer than an active contributor to the production, I can say that the effort required to make this change was worth it. The move shaved more than an hour off our travel time coming and going. The new location was convenient to our favorite hunting and fishing spots too. Perhaps the best part was the view. The same thing said to matter most about real estate also applies to duck swamps: location, location, location.

"No question is so difficult to answer as that to which the answer is obvious."
~ George Bernard Shaw

To Hunt or Not

"Why do you like hunting so much, Pop?" The question

weighed me down as some of my grade school friends were pestering me about killing animals for sport. It was not easy to answer them as the pat retort was always, "You don't have to *kill* these days to eat."

Pop considered the question. He closed his eyes, turned his bearded face to the intensely blue sky this early November day to formulate what I knew would be *the* answer. Pop was anything but indecisive. I was sure he would arm me with the ultimate comeback to my schoolmates' constant ridicule.

"Son, it's like this. There are many reasons I enjoy hunting. You see, it's not just about killing animals…hold that thought." He went back to scanning the tree lines for incoming ducks.

It was almost late afternoon in the Brambles, several miles up the swamp from the houseboat. We lay hidden next to a leaning cypress that jutted from a clump of its kind, utilizing the natural screen of Spanish moss hanging from its furry branches.

Duck season would open in just a few weeks. We were at Santee to find places the birds frequented so we could return to them when the season began. Also, we were putting the finishing touches on a duck blind in a slough near the houseboat. We carried two-by-fours, plywood, a handsaw, hammer, and nails in the boat this trip. Earlier in the day, I held the wood up in a cypress tree while the boat bobbed so Pop could nail the frame together. I was learning that there was nothing easy about successful duck hunting.

In a low voice, Pop finally continued, "There are always going to be folks who don't understand why people would want to hunt. Going back into history, Man has always hunted. It's called survival. Didn't I see you studying Darwin's Theory of Evolution earlier this school year?"

"Yes, sir." I also recently recalled a heated discussion over dinner where Mommy and Pop chimed in concerning Darwin's opinions.

Duck Tale

Pop's view got the submarine treatment. Momma sank his battleship quite handily by shouting, "God created man in His image! You may be descended from a monkey, but I'm sure not!" She went to the kitchen, where clattering arose from her starting to clean up after dinner. She certainly didn't like the school undermining her hard work raising me to be a Christian. I realized it was my turn to do the dishes, and I was getting out of it. Heh, heh, heh.

Since Pop had brought up the subject again this afternoon, I prepared for a very in-depth explanation. "Your mother and I have differing viewpoints about the Creation versus Darwinism. Darwin believed that humans developed over millions of years of Evolution. Your mother holds a Christian fundamentalist view. She believes

Pair of Wood Ducks
The male is most colorful, while the female is somewhat drab. This image is the work of a U.S. Fish and Wildlife Service employee, taken or made as part of that person's official duties. As a work of the U.S. federal government, the image is in the public domain.

that God literally created the world in six twenty-four-hour days and rested on the seventh – not millions of years, and certainly not from apes. Here come some ducks. Shhhhhh..."

To my disappointment, we had to pause in this fruitful discussion. A flight of ducks was landing a hundred yards out in front of us. With little webbed feet spread, the V-formation swiftly dropped toward the water to skim the surface before settling down. They floated around the pigweed with their perfectly adapted feather bodies – Darwinism in the flesh. Ducks must be the latest rendition in a string of evolutionary mutations that dated back to the leathery pterodactyls with their giant wingspans.

After a while, Pop turned back to the discussion in a quiet voice, "I think God is not limited by Time. I think His days could last as long or as short as He sees fit. So, what if His Plan took millions of years? Those years, to God, are but moments. I think both Darwin and Christians are right. Look, look. Here come some wood ducks. See the colorful feathers on the male? Notice the dull brown on all the others? Those are the females."

Despite myself, I got sidetracked from the discussion. "Why are the females so drab while the males are so handsome?"

"God made them that way. Or perhaps He let Evolution take a hand. All I know is that women sure primp in front of a handsome man like your daddy. Do you know how babies are made?"

Now, how did *that* come up? I felt the heat of embarrassment rising in my cheeks.

Pop frowned. "I see you've had a bit of sex education. Don't let your mother know, or she'll tear that school apart. We signed a paper declining to have you taught that subject in elementary school."

"We only skimmed through the human anatomy part while talking about Evolution." I thought that would end this uncomfortable subject. How wrong I was! Somehow, our dialogue of why hunting was crucial to Pop got waylaid, and I couldn't figure out how.

Pop mowed on. "Do you know about the Birds and the Bees?"

I flushed.

"Okie Dokie. Since you've been shown how babies are made, I'll skip right to the important details. After all, it's my duty as a father to make sure you understand what you will be growing into soon. I know you'll find it rough discussing this with me, but actually, this is the perfect time, the perfect spot, and the perfect way to explain hunting."

My mouth dropped as he described in most graphic detail the workings of a man and a woman. Reading a paragraph and viewing genitalia in a Science text simply doesn't do the subject any justice. I forgot all about the ducks.

"So, Boy, now that you know, keep that thing in your pants. Is that clear?"

I nodded. "Yes, sir." My mind was in turmoil, but one thing was sure: I would keep my *thing* in my pants. I recalled how everyone in the class had burst out laughing when the teacher muddled through the information. Oh yes, my *thing* was safely tucked away for the time being.

"Now that we've had the *discussion*, I want you to notice how the subject of hunting is related. You see, until recent history, Man had to hunt to survive. Hunting for food is part of our very nature, the same as making babies. This is how God ensured the *survival* of His Creation. From the scientific point of view, we could say that we evolved to survive in a harsh environment by growing smarter. It's smart to have tools like guns so we can shoot our food. Guns are better than clubs, don't you think?"

I nodded affirmatively.

"Besides eating and mating, God also made us expel waste and sleep. So, there it is in a nutshell: we eat, sleep, poop, and mate. God made us this way so we can survive as a species. It's called the Human Condition. Evolution may have brought us to where we are today. Still, I believe God created Evolution as the driving force to keep his Creation going."

That was deep. "So, Pop, I still don't understand why hunting is so important to *you*." It was my feeble attempt to track back to my original question.

Pop stole a sidelong glance at me from under his thick brows before continuing to search the skies for ducks. "Boy, I think you'll figure it out if you'll stick with me. The Bible tells us that God created Man, male and female, in His image on the Sixth Day. He gave mankind dominion over the whole earth. I would say He covered all the bases, wouldn't you?"

"Yes, sir." Although he lost me there.

"You know I grew up on a farm during a time when people raised cows and chickens, planted vegetable gardens, and processed food themselves. Grandmother and Granddaddy still do. Every year they plant a big garden and can a lot of vegetables. They don't rely on the grocery store for everything they eat. That way of living comes from having grown up in tough times. Your grandparents take care of themselves. They are survivors, no matter what may come along. I am training you to be a survivor too. I want you to know how to feed yourself and your family if hard times come again. The biggest step is learning how to use your head and *not* let those snotty-nosed kids at school sway your thinking. Never forget that. Your mind is your greatest tool, given by God, so you can learn to survive anything that may come down the pike."

"A gun is also a tool. It can be used to *murder*, or it can be used to *kill*. There is a big difference between the two. We hunters use our tools to kill animals, but that is not the same as murder, no matter what those touchy-feely little friends of yours may think. Man learned to protect himself from lions and tigers and bears with weapons, but he also learned to make war, and out of anger, murder other men. Guns are not just weapons. They help provide food. In your semester report from your teacher, I read that you studied hunting and gathering societies like Neanderthal Man, so you understand what I'm saying, right? It's natural for us to kill to survive – Survival of the Fittest. It's not natural to murder. That comes from uncontrolled hatred and anger. Hunters don't get upset about shooting animals for food."

"But...but Pop," I was trying to wrap my head around the subject, "my friends say we don't have to hunt to survive anymore. They make fun of me for being a hunter. They say that hunters do nothing but murder Bambis." Disney had just aired their animated film, *Bambi*, last week on primetime television, so all the kids were discussing it. My homeroom teacher had told us that the movie was based on a book from nineteen-twenty-three by someone named Felix Salten and that Salten had been a hunter. It did no good pointing that out to my classmates.

"That's because they don't understand the subject. Why do you think I started so far back in history to help you understand the importance of hunting?"

"I'm not sure."

"Because the answer isn't simple. You must learn the answer for yourself using your own brain. I suppose you've noticed how I keep approaching the matter from different angles. Hold on, here come some more birds." He hunched down for a better view through the moss.

Ducks in flight are fascinating creatures, I mused. Why would anyone want to shoot them out of the sky? What if my friends were right? We don't need ducks for food. There's always plenty of food on the table, three meals a day, and in-between snacks too. My head was swirling.

The sun was getting low behind us, an orange ball tinged red where it sank toward the horizon. Soon it would be time to go back to the houseboat. I hoped we would be leaving shortly. I hated traveling through the swamp in the dark. The stumps could overturn the boat, or sink us, or we could get lost in the darkness, or –

"Hey, Boy! Pay attention. I've been talking to you. Did you hear what I said?"

"No, sir."

"I said it's time to go. We've got the rest of the weekend to finish this discussion. Let's go get some supper, and then I'll teach you how to catch catfish! Sound good? Now, hand me a beer."

I dutifully opened the camouflaged cooler and handed him a Bud. Pop had painted it olive drab to hide the safety-orange plastic from the ducks' keen eyes. Earlier, he had let me take a small sip just to see what beer tasted like. It was disgusting. Yucky stuff!

We readied for departure, untangling streamers of moss from the paddles as we pushed our way out of our natural duck blind. The boat slid easily into open water once Pop lifted the motor's prop from the clump of pigweed that had held us in place for the last several hours. Pigweed was thick, effortlessly ripped from underwater moorings by wind and current, and moved around. This made navigation more interesting, especially at night. The waterscape would appear mysteriously different than earlier the same day.

🦆🦆🦆🦆🦆🦆🦆🦆🦆

As darkness descended, my apprehension grew. Pop pulled out the choke, jerked the starter cord several times, with no success. He pushed the choke in to prevent too much gas from flooding the carburetor, yanked the starter cord once more, and with the customary roar of a combustion engine, we were off to the houseboat. I was just glad the motor started.

Pop yelled over the noise, "Just look at all the ducks!" He was pointing with his free hand at several hundred birds lifting all around us in the dusk. His face was alight with excitement. "This is where we're gonna hunt at Thanksgiving! Can you believe how many of them sneaked in on us while we talked? Wait till Vee Bee hears about this!"

Settled on the front bench behind the bow, gripping my flashlight in front of me with both hands, I peered through my new glasses, searching for obstacles. Pop showed no concern whatsoever about striking anything in the dark. To satisfy me, we worked out a method of signaling that didn't involve pointing. Pointing got confusing – begging questions like "What's he pointing at? A stump? A snake? A low branch?" Usually, it was too late to make any course adjustment if a stump was coming. The boat would make an almighty lurch. Everything would shift, including me, and the swamp would come close to spilling over one side or the other. Then we'd most likely get stuck and have the move everything around to free ourselves and get underway. It was a new experience, scary to me. Need I say more?

The signal system was straightforward. "Lean left or right to tell me which way to go, Boy. Make sure you do it sudden and concise and in plenty of time for me to turn." I felt silly jerking left and right in my seat, but it worked.

There was a procedure that developed over time as we learned to live in the homemade hut. Once the boat was tied off, I climbed onto the porch, unlocked the two padlocks, opened the door, and used my flashlight to locate the battery cables under the bunk. As I reached to connect the wire clamps to the battery posts, something cold and wet crawled across my hand.

I yelped and leaped back.

"What's the matter, Boy? You trying to take a swim?"

I looked wildly at my boots to see that I was indeed about to step off into the water. "P-pop, something ran across my hand!"

"T'aint nothing but a roach or a spider. Get the lights turned on."

Swallowing my fear, I reached back in and achieved my task placing the cables on the twelve-volt car battery to power the low voltage lighting. I flipped the switch for the light above my head. There, on the floor, was the fattest lizard I had ever seen. A lizard. Big deal.

"It's just a lizard, Pop."

"He must've come in to hibernate through the winter. Toss him out."

"But won't he die?"

"Nah. He'll find another warm spot somewhere. Would you rather step on him in the dark?"

I scooped him up and tossed him out the door toward the nearest cypress. Checking my Timex, the watch that "takes a licking and keeps on ticking," I discovered that it was only 6:30 P.M. After all the excitement, it felt like midnight. We had arrived in a flurry to get into the Brambles and look for ducks before dark. I didn't have a snack or a drink all afternoon.

"What's for dinner, Pop?" Visions of Cub Scout hobo burgers and hotdogs washed between my ears. I could smell them, taste them, but they were imaginary. You can't eat a mirage.

"It isn't going to be much, Boy." He paused his rummaging in the cooler to look me in the eye. "Hunter's Rule #1: Eat what you shoot. Hunter's Rule #2: If you don't catch it or shoot it, you don't eat. Hunter's Rule #3: What happens at Santee stays at Santee. Hunter's Rule #4: If you're on time, you're late. Hunter's Rule #5: See all of the above." He chuckled and went back to rummaging. This did not bode well for my empty stomach.

Inside the Houseboat

"Hey Pop, what does Hunter's Rule #4 mean?"

"It means that if you're going hunting, and you agree to be at a certain place at a certain time, you need to be there early. There's so much to do to get the car loaded. If you are on time and only start loading up then, you'll probably get to the swamp too late to shoot. The same goes for other activities. Besides, you don't want people standing around waiting on a slowpoke when there's hunting to be done. I know people who've been left behind. I've had to leave 'em myself." He finished pulling food out of the cooler.

Hungry as I was, the cold SpaghettiOs were a feast. Fritos and French onion dip went well with them too. Twinkies made a great dessert. Then, it was time to go catfishing. I had no clue what that would involve.

"Don't think I've forgotten our discussion," said Pop. "When we get back from setting the catfish hooks, we'll get something to drink and sit out here on the porch to watch the stars. We'll talk some more then. Right now, make sure you have your knife and the cutting board. Crawl back in the boat."

And so, I gave Pop the customary, "Yes, sir," patted my sheathed skinning knife on my hip, grabbed the cutting board from under the bunk, and climbed aboard the boat.

We were off again, only this time we were fishing. Once we scooted back up to Long Pond, Pop started searching for low overhanging limbs. I had no idea why.

"There's a good one. I'm going to cut the motor. When I do, you grab the limb and hold whatcha got." I was dubious about this action. However, after doing it another thirty times within an hour, I became an expert.

Each time the motor stopped, the procedure would be the same:

Step One. I tied the bow rope to a limb so we wouldn't float away.

Step Two. Pop would pass me a four-foot length of nylon string to which a large, heavy-duty, stainless steel fishhook was attached. I mean a big hook!

"Pop, why's the hook so large?"

"Wait till you see the size of the mouth that grabs it, Boy. Now keep on with business. We haven't got all night."

Step Three. While avoiding the hook, which now rested on my bluejeaned knee, I would cut yet another two-inch chunk of truly rotten, stinking mullet off a carcass. This fish had been left to putrefy all day on the bow in the sun.

"Ugh. Pop? Why do we have to use rotten fish to catch catfish?"

"Good question. Answer: because catfish were designed to clean up the bottom of the waterways. They eat whatever dead food they can get their mouths around. They comb the bottom, rooting around for whatever fish poop, bird poop, animal carcasses, or dead turtles –

anything they can find. Just think what the swamp would be like if catfish didn't clean up that sort of stuff. They're like buzzards of the lake. We'd be up to our asses – I mean – eyeballs in doo-doo, wouldn't we?" As an aside, he added, "Don't forget. What happens at Santee stays at Santee." In the transom light's glow, I caught a wink. Privately, I hoped that catfish tasted a whole lot better than this rotten mullet smelled.

Step Four was not too complicated. It was merely to bait the hook. I proceeded to stab the hunk of meat as Pop readjusted himself on his boat cushion. I shoved the hook home – right into my palm – because the boat rocked unexpectedly.

"YEEEOOWW!"

"Sorry, Boy. My butt's getting tired. Hurry up and finish that last hook and let's get back to the houseboat."

I extracted the hook from my palm, with blood pouring from the puncture. "Pop, I'm bleeding." And yes, it hurt.

"That's okay. Catfish love blood. Make sure some of it gets on that bait. I'll bet this line catches the monster fish." Snickering followed.

Step Five. This entailed picking up the hunk of bait and putting it on the hook correctly. Catfish, I learned, would mouth their food before sucking it into their gullet. They could work the bait loose unless the hook was stuck well into the mullet's skin or even a piece of bone. Like the other twenty-nine hooks, I completed my task and gently dropped it in the water, so the line hung straight down, suspended by the pliable limb above.

Step Six. I rinsed my hands in swamp water to get the stench and blood off without spreading it to my clothing.

Step Seven. I picked up my paddle and gently pushed us away from the tree.

Step Eight. Pop started the motor, and we idled our way back through Long Pond, checking each of the thirty lines to make sure that none were tangled.

Finally, after about an hour, we got back to the houseboat for our drink and relaxation on the porch. Pop had already mentioned that we would go out to check the catfish lines at 11:00 P.M., so we could talk for the next hour or so about hunters. I was okay with sitting on the porch to view the stars while we spoke.

"Boy, the fact is, not everyone is built for hunting. People these days are too squeamish. Now take what happened to you a little while ago. You stuck yourself with that hook, right? Bled too, and it hurt, but you didn't start crying and acting like a baby or passing out from the sight of blood. I'm proud of you. How many of your friends would have done the same?"

"I don't know, Pop. Not many?"

"That's right – not many. Hunters get hurt. Fishermen get hurt. Everyone gets hurt from time to time, but outdoorsmen don't whine about it. No matter how bad they may get hurt, they still have to walk out of the wilderness. They just clean themselves up, get a bandage, and push on. Never forget that, Son. You still have to walk out; otherwise, *you die.*"

That was a pearl of wisdom if I ever heard one. I stared up at the endless heavens, silently considering Pop's admonition. *You still have to walk out; otherwise, you die.* The proverbial lightbulb blazed inside my skull.

Pop continued, "I've heard all the arguments against hunting, but let me tell you, without hunters, there would be no ducks, no doves, no turkeys, no deer, no nothing left to shoot. Did you know that hunters, through licensing fees, pay for virtually all the conservation efforts that go on to try and save the wetlands for the ducks? Without hunters, the wetlands would not be preserved, so the ducks would fly elsewhere for food and shelter."

Duck Tale

Pop was on a roll now. My head was beginning to fill up.

"You've read stories about the Indians, right? Good. I'll bet those stories told you how the Indians went out to hunt for game animals like deer and buffalo to feed their families. If they didn't *thin* the herds by killing off some of the animals to eat, make clothing, and create tools, many animals would have starved. That's right. Nature is a juggling act. It's called the Balance of Nature. A certain amount of land can support only so many animals. If animals become too numerous for the food supply and land available to them, they will starve and die. And people are part of that process. If too many people are in an area, they will starve unless new food supplies can be obtained. That's why Indians were nomads. They moved around in search of more food sources after they had hunted out an area. Once they moved on, the animals would come back and increase the population again. Hunters today are Conservationists at heart, not at all like the Indians were. We want to keep the herds healthy. One way to do that is to thin them out when necessary; otherwise, they'd starve to death through overpopulation. That would be wasteful, wouldn't you say? Wouldn't it be better to hunt the animals to keep the herds healthy and eat what you take rather than waste the meat?"

Now, this was a new way of looking at hunting. So far, all I had comprehended was that people went out into the woods and swamps to kill animals. Things were beginning to make sense. "But, Pop, what about cows, chickens, and such? We buy them at the grocery store anytime we want. We don't have to go out and kill them ourselves."

"That's true. I'm sure some of those friends of yours are only considering that one point. I bet none of them have ever been hunting. Maybe they've been fishing. Fishing's the same type of thing. The same rules apply. But for some reason, people don't go all squeamish over fish guts as they do over animal guts. I suppose it's because warm-blooded creatures remind us too much of ourselves – like when you saw your own blood. Didn't you feel a bit queasy when you first saw that hook planted in your skin?"

"I sure did. Then I remembered what you told me about men not crying every time they get hurt. It stung, but not enough to make me cry."

"That's exactly what I'm saying. Your friends, most of them anyway, will never understand what it means to be a hunter because they've never done it and probably never will. They'll just buy their processed meat from the grocery without ever understanding what it means to fend for themselves. It's more important to know how to feed yourself off the land if there's no food at the grocery store. It can happen. People have starved throughout history. Like you're learning in Scouts, it's best to be prepared. Now back to the Indians. Did your book describe a hunt?"

"Yes, sir, it did."

"Well then, I've read lots of Indian books in my time. Indians were serious hunters. They only killed what they needed to survive, right?"

"Yes, sir."

"Did the book also tell you that Indians revered their quarry? That means they held in high regard the value of that animal's life. Many tribes had rituals to thank their Great Spirits for a successful hunt. Others believed in thanking the animal's spirit for giving up its life so they could feed their families."

"The book certainly did, Pop." As I gazed up at the stars, I realized my dad was a very knowledgeable man. He knew exactly what I was going through at school. He also knew that there was nothing he could tell me in a nutshell that would make me understand why hunting was so important to him. My father was a frontiersman at heart. I had been reading a biography of Daniel Boone and his dealings with the Shawnee Nation. Everything Pop was saying was in that book. What a wonder!

"That book is lying, Son. Indians didn't care about being conservative. They were just feeding their families. They killed out the game in one area, then moved on to another. They were even worse farmers. They didn't know anything about soil conservation or modern farming. Their goal was to survive. If you haven't studied slash-and-burn agriculture yet in school, you will. A more accurate view of how primitive peoples lived is to understand they did what they had to do to live." He took a big breath, "We've had a long talk, and we'll get some more in tomorrow. It's time to check the catfish lines. If a limb is bobbing, that means we've caught something. Take your paddle, run it up behind the line as we slide up to the tree, pull the string over, and grab it. Plop that fish into the boat quickly, so it doesn't have time to wriggle off the hook. I'll be helping you the first time or two."

So off we went again into the night up to Long Pond. It was a good night too. Excitement coursed through me as I saw the first bouncing line come into the light of my torch. The entire limb had bent down into the water and was twisting around and jerking up and down. We had caught something big!

"Would ya look at that, Boy? We got one! Get ready with your paddle. Here, I'm coming over." The boat listed as Pop's weight came down beside me. He leaned to grab the string when I hooked and drew it over with my paddle. Limbs above swished across our hats as the whole boat slipped toward the tree. "Holy Cow, this is one big fish! Help me lift him into the boat, Son!"

The water was somewhat murky, so my flashlight's feeble beam didn't penetrate very far into the depths. I dropped my paddle into the boat to free my hand to help with the line and still keep the flashlight trained on the spot.

Then, it happened.

A mouth that seemed a foot wide rose to the surface under our combined efforts to lift the fish into the boat. It nearly scared the crap out of me! Oh, pardon the French. What stays at Santee, well, you know the rest by now. Pop pressed his knees against the side of the boat to get better leverage. He landed a regular, flopping, fighting, surging, slimy pig with fins into the bottom with one enormous heave. I'd never seen a fish that big except on television. I'd also never imagined the havoc giant catfish could wreak in small watercraft.

First, the bait bucket was overthrown, sending chum everywhere, but mostly all over us. Next, the cooler toppled over. Our ice for the weekend poured across the bottom under our feet, along with a couple of gallons of water and cold drinks. Pop struggled with the line, trying to get the hook from the mouth of the monster. I could see that it had been swallowed deep into the back of the gaping maw. I also saw rows of tiny little teeth along the gums, much like I had seen in pictures of sharks, only not nearly as large.

"Boy, I've got him by the fins. Now stick your hand down in there and get that hook loose."

I had to drop the flashlight, but the transom light was still emitting enough of a glow to see this operation through. "Won't he bite my hand?"

"No. No. He can't hurt you. Now get in there and get that hook. When you get it loose, make sure to release it over the side of the boat well away from us. I don't want either of us to get a hook in the eye!"

"Yes, sir." Gritting my teeth, I plunged my hand down that catfish's throat, grabbed that hook, worked it free, and plopped the hook back in the water in one smooth motion. I was masterful.

"That's great! Aaaaahhh..." The catfish flopped away toward the back of the boat, levitating like a dog going for a treat. In the dimness, I could see dark blood welling from Pop's palm where the fin, barely more than a boney spike, had sliced him open like a knife. "Ummmmph..." Pop added.

I looked at his face. He wore one of those grimaces people get when they've hurt themselves doing something stupid. Though he obviously found it painful, the situation with the fish beating up the boat, the blood going everywhere, and his expression were just too much for one day.

I laughed. Respectfully. I couldn't help it. Mirth bubbled up from the depths of my being.

"What're you laughing at, Boy?" I could tell Pop was not angry. He turned to the swamp water as I had done earlier, rinsed his hand, and turned back to tackle that catfish once again. He slammed his boot up against the body of the struggling fish, pinning it against the backbench. Although the fish still struggled, we both sighed in relief. "That's one *big* fish, Boy. Not bad for your first time. We've still got twenty-nine hooks to check. Maybe the others won't be so dramatic."

I laughed some more. Sure enough, we hauled in quite a bounty. Before midnight we had strung eighteen catfish through the gills onto a nylon rope. Each was better than seven pounds. The first catfish, the one that ripped Pop open, weighed in at twenty-two. What a monster!

"There now. We've strung 'em all out so we can clean 'em up for stew. We'll get to it tomorrow morning. Looks like we'll have to make a run back to the landing for more ice, though."

"But Pop, won't the fish die like that?" I watched the stringer, which was tied off to one of the cleats mounted on the porch, making lazy circles as the catfish swam around beneath us.

"No. Catfish are hard to kill. They're in the cold water, breathing like normal. They'll be as lively tomorrow and even next week if we leave 'em like that. Boy, not only are we gonna have the best stew you ever put in your mouth, but we're also gonna take home a cooler full of fish to last the rest of the year! We'd better get cleaned up, brush teeth, and hop in bed. Tomorrow's gonna be another big day!"

"Happiness is not a destination. It is a method of life."
~ Burton Hillis

Another Big Day

The houseboat was cozy, sure. Pop was careful that everything had a place and was appropriately stowed. That included people. I was a person.

"Git up, Boy! It's time to go out and watch for ducks." It was

5:00 A.M. Pop had been banging around for the last fifteen minutes, gloriously awake. He was prepping our standard warmer-upper for cold mornings – a thermos of Campbell's Cream of Mushroom Soup – coupled with another thermos of scalding coffee. "Don't forget to bring your cup so you can have some soup later. You might want to grab a milk carton since you're too young for coffee." Yeah, I was still too young for adult beverages.

With reluctance, I unzipped my warm sleeping bag and crawled out of the top bunk. Not wanting to forget my pint of milk, I put the carton in the big pocket of my jacket. I'd have to be careful not to bust it. "How cold do you think it is, Pop?"

"Why don't you stick your head out and see, Boy? I'm not a weatherman."

That sounded like a good idea. I didn't want to overdress, nor did I desire to underdress and be cold all morning. Slipping out the front door to the porch, I took the opportunity to relieve myself away from the prying eyes of my father. He never missed a trick, though. The boat had started rocking, of course. "POP!"

"Haaahhaaah."

I was standing out in thick wool socks, sporting my full-length, cotton thermal underwear. Even so, the damp chill of early morning crept into my bones. I couldn't resist staring out into the dark wilderness and listening to the tiny sounds of the swamp preparing to awaken.

A limb plopped in the water nearby, or perhaps it was a fish of some sort breaking the surface. Far off, an owl hooted mournfully, apparently having no mate to respond in kind. Pop was shoving things around inside. Over those sharp noises, I distinctly heard tiny splish-splashes not too far off toward Long Pond. I wondered if those strangely rhythmic plops could be catfish tugging at the lines.

"Boy! Git back in here and git ready to go! The sun will come up soon. We need to be in place before then."

"Coming." I slid back in the door and quickly dressed in the usual camo outfit. It was cold enough to warrant my heavy insulated outer jacket too. I threw it on, milk and all.

Pop rumbled toward me with an armload. "Take some of this stuff to the boat."

"Yes, sir." I took the two thermoses under one arm and offered to carry his new insulated acquisition, a thermal cup. He thrust a couple of spoons into my outer breast pocket. I had already stuffed my own Scout mess kit cup into my front hip pocket next to the milk.

"Hurry up, now. We don't have far to go, just behind us, but I want to put out some decoys and hopefully test my new duck call. I let you sleep too late!"

Getting my boat legs under me, a matter of balance, I stepped off into the middle section and began taking the gear Pop handed down to me. All the while, the porch light was burning. I noticed it was dimmer than it had been last night.

"Is the battery going to run out of juice before we get home, Pop?"

"Nah. It'll be fine. We've only got tonight left anyway. Take this." A sizeable olive-drab canvas duffle slammed into my arms, weighted heavily with decoys. I could feel the knobby Styrofoam heads of the fake birds pressing through the bag against my thigh. Since I had never put out decoys before, I didn't know what would be involved.

Soon we had all the accouterments we needed for scouting birds. Pop got the motor warmed up. It was still dark. Since we were alone, and since we were not going out to the big water, we did not install the bow and transom lights. The half-moon offered all the light we needed to navigate.

As the crisp, clean air brought me fully awake, yesterday's deliberations about hunting were revived too. Today – Saturday – would probably allow Pop to finish sharing his wisdom on the subject. For now, the silken water offered safe passage without bumpy interruptions.

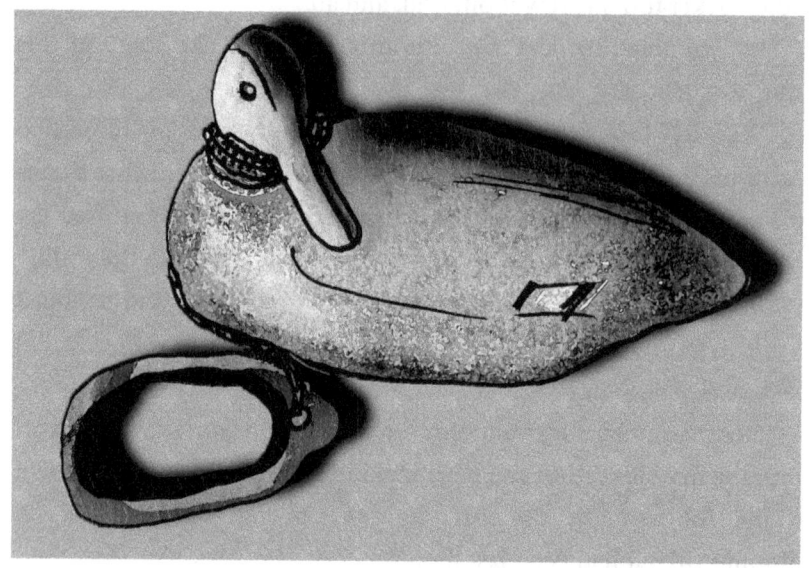

Female Mallard Decoy with Anchor Ring

Not far behind the houseboat, our trail opened into a private little slough lined with trees. Several stumps reared their heads out in the middle, but one on the port side showed promise as a mooring while we awaited the sunrise. It was a burned-out husk, the remains after one massive lightning strike. The trunk laid over where it had broken off, aligned with the slough. Pop decided to drop the decoys in between the tree line and this stump. When the sun appeared, we would be facing it.

"Now, here's what we're gonna do," Pop began as he cut the motor and allowed us to drift into the middle of open water. "Reach in the bag and toss me a decoy. I'm gonna show you how to handle 'em."

I unclasped the Army surplus duffle's carry strap, and several decoys spilled out at my feet. I reached for the first one, a gray female mallard. It was made of foam and had a gray head with a dingy yellow beak that swiveled. Around the head was wrapped several feet of green nylon cord tied to a rough oval hoop made of lead. It had been slipped over the decoy's head for storage. The line was tied off to an O-ring on the decoy's bottom. I supposed the lead would act like an anchor, preventing the decoy from floating away. As I handed the fake duck over to Pop, my deduction was confirmed.

Pop slipped the anchor from the head, carefully uncoiled the cord from around the neck, and gently tossed the contraption lead-first about four feet out from the boat. This sounds most boring; however, correct placement is vital if you want to fool the real thing into dropping from the sky.

"Boy, your turn. You get the decoys and toss 'em where I point. Try to keep the noise to a minimum. You never can tell how many of those ducky-blats are already here."

"Yes, sir." I started the project while Pop guided us slowly around with his paddle. He was using combinations of *J-strokes* and *sweep strokes* to ease us into new positions. These techniques, standard for canoers and kayakers, work well for jon boats too.

Soon I had tossed out thirteen mallard decoys. There were six green-headed drakes intermixed with an odd number of females.

"Hey, Pop, how do you know where to put all these things?"

"Easy." He paddled us out from among the newly placed decoys and over to the burned stump. "We scatter the decoys in such a way that they sit the area naturally, like the real birds. When they get moved by the water current or a breeze, they'll look active. If we don't place them properly, they can get tangled, a real mess to pick up."

"Okay, so why did we put out an odd number?"

"Ducks mate for life. An odd number means a single bird might find a spouse. It'll lure 'em in to fill the gap."

I pondered that. Hmmm...must be another one of those embarrassing male-female relationship subjects like we discussed yesterday. My gut told me it didn't really matter what combination of decoys we dropped out, but Pop sure could devise an answer to any question. I decided to leave it alone.

Using the motor briefly to push us into a pile of pigweed surrounding the stump, he expertly placed us against the fallen trunk. Like at the Brambles last night, the mossy limbs helped conceal us on the sunward side. Starboard was another matter. We were wide open.

"Git out the camo bag from upfront."

Moonlight was more than sufficient for this minor operation. I reached over the front bench to draw forth another canvas bag, much lighter than the decoys, and handed it to Pop. He pulled out great wads of camouflaged cloth, all odd sizes but made of sturdy materials. We draped the fabric over the boat's full length, allowing it to fall around haphazardly, even into the water. It got soaked and hung heavily. Some pieces even got strung up in the limbs of the fallen tree. The entire starboard edge was now lined in camouflage. Cloth laid about on the mass of pigweed, too, blending our profile seamlessly into Nature.

"It's going to be sunrise soon. Notice the sky lightening through the trees. Get covered up with this cloth. Here, throw some on your shoulders and across your legs. Yeah. Like that. Now the birds won't be able to tell we're sitting here in a boat. We'll look just like the pigweed and a couple of stumps." He fumbled around with one of the thermos bottles. "Gimme your cup." The aroma of the thick mushroom soup drifted by on the moist air making my mouth water. What can I say? I was starving again. A growing boy, you know.

Unexpectedly, a loud squawk issued from Pop's new duck call, nearly causing me to spill my soup. For the past six weeks, he'd been practicing along with a new eight-track tape of professional duck callers demonstrating various calls. It sounded good to me. But what did I know? All around us, I heard tiny pitter-patters as if many small creatures were slapping the water...perhaps with feathers?

The glow of dawn began to spill through the trees.

Eight-Track Tape
From the mid-1960s until the 1980s this cartridge of magnetic sound-recording technology was compact enough so players could be installed in automobiles. It was not for making personal recordings, however. That still had to be done on reel-to-reel tape recorders.

Pop admonished me to sit still and only use my peripheral vision to look around for flying birds. His duck call would blast out a combination of quacks, feed chuckles, and other fancy warbles every so often. I was surprised at all the tones his cigar-shaped wooden device emitted. The call itself operated much the same way as blowing a piece of grass between your thumbs. It has a reed mounted inside a small blowhole. When air from the mouth is forced through, the reed vibrates to create the sound. Using cheek muscles, the palms, and body language, a most convincing replica of duck chatter could be achieved.

Pop was a novice at this point in his duck calling career. The ducks began to fly all right – fly away just as fast as their streamlined wings could carry them. Splashing erupted all around us for another five minutes or so, and then it was all over. The sun was up. The decoys bobbed serenely fifteen yards away, and the quackers were gone. Only brief glimpses of tail feathers awarded our efforts. We sat there freezing our backsides for another two hours. No amount of cajoling with the call lured a single duck.

In the silence of the burgeoning day, I asked, "Why do you like hunting?"

"Don't test me, Boy." He began stuffing the soppy wet cloth into the sack with some vigor. I could tell he was fuming, probably at himself. Becoming a master duck caller took him several more years of hard practice. He went through thirty or forty more duck calls, each a touch different in style and timbre. Then, the hunting was on for real. If it was a duck and wasn't in the mood to stay airborne all day, he could coax it to the decoys. Meanwhile, we had sparse pickings.

In a disgruntled tone, Pop said, "Let's get the decoys in and go check the catfish lines."

"Yes, sir."

I had now discovered that hunting ducks took much time and practice. Those little buggers were smart. Cautious to a fault. It wasn't just a matter of zooming into the swamp for a quick shoot. There was a massive amount of real work involved if one wanted to take a duck. How the Indians could have brought ducks down with bows and arrows, I'll never know. Maybe those stories were just tall tales.

It took several more years of lessons in constraint to successfully match wits with ducks. The first thing to remember is no unnecessary movement, period. Ducks could spot a turn of the head, a flutter of camo in the breeze, or the shift of a tired posterior from a mile

A Few of Pop's Duck Calls

away. The movement of one pale finger on the trigger was sometimes enough to flare incoming *V*-formations of ducks before they ever got within firing range. Ducks can easily detect us for what we are, humans in disguise.

The catfish lines were full again. It was far easier to extract the bounty from the hooks in daylight. I was finned across the meaty part of my thumb, like Pop last night. It burned terribly from the slime that coated the slick skin of the fish.

Yes, catfish are slimy. Their skin, devoid of scales found on other types of fish, is coated with lubricant. A catfish's body is mostly head sporting a few whiskers to each side of a gaping mouth. Those mouths gulp air into gills capable of keeping them alive out of water for many hours. Catfish are ugly, slick slabs of tasty meat.

"So, Pop, why is it you like hunting again?" I was up to my elbows in catfish guts, learning to clean and filet them for the pot. Pop was too.

"Son, haven't you learned anything this trip? Where else can you go for nearly complete privacy? Run around naked if you want? Talk about all kinds of important stuff? Do things you can't repeat when you get home? And, still have fun catching fish and shooting ducks?"

I considered that in silence as I continued pulling slimy skin from a catfish carcass. Cleaning fish was messy, not fun at all, but Pop was right about getting to say and do things down here in the swamp that couldn't be repeated at home. Things like talking about sex, tasting beer for the first time, being worried about hitting stumps, trying to navigate in the fog and the dark, thinking the boat would sink at any moment, hearing owls hooting at night, seeing ducks zooming by so fast they were mostly a blur, putting out decoys, learning to catfish, listening to the sounds of unseen critters during the night, learning about survival, and pain, and...and...*excitement*...beyond my wildest dreams!

The author holding catfish in front of the Leaning Tree in 1976

"Some people are so afraid to die that they never begin to live."
~ Henry Van Dyke

Death Stump

It was cold. Wet. The perfect weekend for hunting ducks. I was thirteen years and a few months old. This was my first time at Santee during actual duck season as a hunter myself. Pop had signed me out of school early so we could get down to the houseboat in time for a quick evening hunt. Mr. Burnett and his son, Brad, were with us. Brad was brown-haired, blue-eyed, and somewhat older and heavier than me – a brawny high schooler. Lately, we had both been invited to join the men on hunts, as gofers, of course.

"Brad, hand me that ammo box, humph, harrumph."

"Yes, Daddy." Brad's voice had changed since I had seen him last. It was deeper, more resonant. Pop had told me that I would also have a lower voice one day soon because I was growing like a weed.

We had been up since 3:00 a.m. eating a heavy breakfast of country ham and eggs with heaps of grits lavished in red-eye gravy, followed by the donning of camouflaged outfits. There was an hour-and-a-half ride up the flats into Sparkleberry Swamp in the dark, another thirty minutes of walk-in across a narrow strip of mud to a duck hidey-hole, and finally a setup of decoys. We should have at least an hour before sunrise to get settled.

Since this was before thermal-insulated specialty gear hit the market, we had quite a procedure. The temperature was about thirty-four, and sleet was pelting the metal roof. We each wore heavy cotton full-length underwear, followed by quilted tops and bottoms, three layers of increasingly thick socks of cotton, polyester, and wool, heavy canvas pants and shirts, extra-thick water-resistant camo hooded jackets, toboggans, and finally, insulated gloves. Oh, but let's not forget the coup de grace: bulky rubber waders that came up to our chests. The pockets of the jackets bulged with flashlights, shotgun shells, wallets with hunting licenses, and duck calls. We were ready to depart the gas-fired warmth of the houseboat.

"Let's git to the boat!" My father was in his element. He lumbered out the door and stepped down into the frigid craft.

"Git the door, Brad," said Vernon.

"Yes, Daddy."

I shuffled past Brad as he padlocked the door. Pop extended his gloved hand for support as I stepped down to sit next to him at the motor. Brad sat down on the middle bench next to his dad.

Purrrrring, ding, ding, ding, went the outboard. Nothing. Pull out the choke. Jerk the starter cord. Purrring, ding, ding, ding, ding. Nothing. "Dammit, Vernon."

"Now, Dick. Don't flood the thing. We don't have time to play with it."

Pop braced himself for another pull. This time, the Evinrude fired up with a smell of unburned oil and gas.

"I told ya not to flood it in the first place."

"Hang on, cause here we go!" Pop reversed us briefly to get away from the houseboat, then slammed the gear into forward, his left glove resting on the tiller and throttle. Immediately the chill air whipped around us and began to penetrate all the insulation. Brad was spotlighting stumps with his flashlight, but he hunkered down and kept the beam fixed straight ahead. Vernon huddled next to him. The two shadowy figures blocked some of the cold air from me. Pop peered ahead in concentration. Stumps slid by unnoticed in the darkness.

At night the trees loomed ominously. I got used to it. I also got used to finding every trail marker possible. It was a navigation technique to keep us from getting lost. "There's the cut, Dick." Vernon vaguely pointed to a small rectangle of white. Sometime in the past, trails through the swamp had been marked with pieces of license plates nailed to trees. Most of the time these markers were above the waterline, easy to spot in the darkness.

Highly reflective license plate rectangles used as trail markers.

"There's Hair Bear stump," said Brad. The boat slipped by a cypress knob covered in lichen and dead weeds like an afro hairstyle. Visions of the silly cartoon bear in *Help! It's the Hair Bear Bunch* aired by CBS on Saturday mornings drifted through my head. He wore hippie clothes and had huge, frizzy yellow hair. I preferred *Johnny Quest* on ABC. It was a bit more serious, a science fiction cartoon.

Pop expertly guided us between trees until the swamp opened into a wide expanse as we headed up Pack's Flats. No further markers were to be seen, but that didn't matter. Our greatest landmarks were visible even in the darkness: The Three Giants. These massive old cypress trees stood like sentinels, far above the rest of the forest. Following trail markers and unique natural features allowed us to avoid many underwater stumps and logs. The trials were clear paths through the swamp.

Let's put this trek in perspective for the layperson. Imagine yourself in the dark trying to navigate in an unfamiliar forest full of roots, logs, and bracken, with a candle. Fill the area with four or five feet of water depth. Now throw in all the things that go bump in the night, but add the reality that things really were bumping our small boat in this shadowy wilderness. The bow light, stern light, and flashlight lit our way. We motored on until we saw the dark outline of the Leaning Tree, pointing out the path leading to the houseboat from the big water of Pack's Flats. Little did I know that the Leaning Tree would take another fifty years to rot and fall. It appeared ready to drop into the swamp at any moment as we slid by on our way up the edge of the cypress line towards Sparkleberry. The wind whipped up a real chill over that expanse of water. We were all cold, teeth chattering, as the sleet turned to large flakes of sloppy snow.

Time slipped towards the coming dawn. The boat jostled and jolted over stumps as we crawled up the lake. Once, we glanced off the edge of a colossal stump just barely poking above the waterline.

Vernon leaned back to say to Pop, "We'd better remember that one, Dick. I didn't see it comin' 'cause it's barely out of the water."

"Sure, Vee Bee. You boys better help me spot those monsters instead of huddling up." Pop was smiling when he said it. He gave me a wink.

After another hour, we finally made our way through the twisty paths to the duck hidey-hole. Flashlights came out of pockets. We barely had an hour to traipse through the mucky woods carrying guns, ammo, sacks of decoys, and other small sundries to get set for the morning hunt before official sunrise. The snow kept coming down to whiten our path to the walk-in swamp. We trudged along over mucky roots, dead plugs of grasses and weeds, broken stumps and logs, and low-hanging moss that slapped our masked faces with tiny icicles. I was hindmost, struggling with the weight of my gear, wishing the exertion would end. During that brief journey, I worked up a sweat.

In a muffled, low voice, Pop said, "We're here. Make as little noise as possible so we don't scare any ducky-blats that have bedded down for the night. Rick – that means you. In fact, you stick with me, and I'll tell you where to stand. Okay, Brad, you go that way. Vernon, you head up there. I'll take the middle with Rick."

Everyone began to move slowly into the swamp, breaking through two-inch-thick ice with every step. The bigger guys were up to their waists, coattails getting wet. Being much lighter even with my load of gear, my steps didn't sink into the muddy bottom as deeply. Even through the waders and all the insulation I wore, the chill began to creep into my bones.

Pop turned to me and whispered, "Here ya go, Boy. A nice stump surrounded by pigweed just for you. Let's prop you right here." He lent me his forearm as a brace while I struggled to rise out of the water enough to sit on the stump. The dead tendrils of pigweed resisted my efforts, but I was in position after several moments of struggle. "Don't make any noise, or you'll frighten the ducks. Stay still, no fidgeting. I'll come and get you when the hunt's over. Don't speak unless it's an emergency."

"Yes, sir. How long will that be?"

"Hours yet. Keep your eyes open for the birds. Wait till they're close enough to shoot. If you get one, mark it with your eyes because we won't go retrieve the birds till after the shoot." With those last instructions, Pop slogged away.

I watched his back sinking deeper into the water until the darkness left only the sloshing of his passage. Snow was still drifting down, specks landing on my thighs and shoulders. I was grateful to be mostly out of the icy water. I could hear the plop of decoys being thrown out from three different directions. After a few more minutes, all noises stopped.

In the silence, my mind alert like never before, I waited for something to happen. At first, there was a lightening of my surroundings until I could see dead trees, plugs of grasses, brambles, broken logs, stumps – all covered in a thin layer of ice dusted with snow. Ice was already freezing around my shins too.

The perimeter of my sight grew by the moment. I became aware of an earthy mustiness in the air through my frozen nostrils. A gloved finger rose to scratch the tip of my nose and broke off tiny icicles. The moisture in the corners of my eyes froze and had to be wiped. As the light grew, reflecting off the ice and smattering of snow, I could almost hear the soundless energy of the sunrise. With the increasing ambiance came tiny splashes accompanied by muffled squawks. The ducks were stirring somewhere in front of me.

Suddenly, the whistling of wings filled the air. Dark shapes passed overhead, streaking toward the unseen sun. Low-lying cloud cover confirmed there would be no sunshine today, but all the same, I knew the sun was rising. So did the ducks. I readied my Harrington and Richardson Topper Jr. Model 490 20-gauge single shot, preparing to flip the hammer back with my thumb and bring it to my cheek. Now more wings whistled. I could make out V-shaped formations flying low around the perimeter against the surrounding tree lines.

BLAM. BLAM, BLAM, BLAM, KA-BLAM!

Everyone else was shooting. My head spun around in all directions as I sought a target. I wriggled around to see behind me. The echoes of the shotguns rolled away over the watery mirror for several seconds, then died out. The ducks had risen up out of the swamp and were gone. My teeth were chattering uncontrollably. It was about 7:00 a.m.

For another hour, ducks sailed across the swamp in tight formations. None came within shooting distance for me. Brad felled two birds. Pop another three. I couldn't see Mr. Burnett's side of the swamp as he was behind me. I was getting impatient, especially since I was freezing. My legs had gone to sleep, and I couldn't feel my toes. I longed to get out of the cold water. Around 9:00 a.m., Pop whistled at last. It brought me out of the lethargy that was creeping through my mind.

After an interminable length of time, I heard the others gathering up their downed birds, stuffing their decoys back in their sacks, and struggling toward the bank. Pop hove into view, breaking a new trail through the ice.

"Let's go, Boy. Follow right behind me. It'll be easier on you."

It was still heavily overcast, so he probably couldn't see me very well. My teeth were chattering, so I only nodded. Gratefully I slipped off the stump. It seemed the water level had risen a few inches since we walked in. I had to hold my shotgun above my head to keep it out of the water.

I was within sight of the bank when it happened. Both my feet slid under a submerged log – first right, then the left. For a moment, I held steady. Then, to my horror, I gradually sank forward until frigid water spilled over the lip of my waders. Cold knives sliced all the way down to my toes. I tried to yell for Pop, but it was too late. My head dropped below the surface, hat drifting away, gun held in a death grip all the way to the muddy bottom. I couldn't right myself.

An eternity passed in murky darkness until a firm hand caught the back of my jacket and raised me out of the water. I felt myself being pulled inexorably, gun still in my hands, as if by a tow truck. Next, I was supine on the ground with muddy water gushing from my mouth. I couldn't think or speak. Every muscle screamed in agony; I was stiffening into a useless, shuddering plank. Pop turned me over on my stomach and gave my back a couple of hard shoves. More water spewed out of me.

"Vernon! Brad! Help me get him outta these waders!"

Strong hands grabbed my ankles. Swiftly, I was turned upside down and being shaken out of my waders. I slipped to the mud. Uncontrollable shaking overtook my senses. Pop stood me back up and began to alternately rub and slap my extremities. Water streamed down my legs into my wool socks. Even in my misery, I knew there would be no way to get warm and dry.

Somehow words escaped through my chattering teeth. "C..c...c..an I g-g-get oooout of m-mmm-my c-c-clothes?" I tried to clamp my mouth shut, but it was futile.

"No, Son. You'll be warmer like you are till we get back. Vernon, we've got to get him to the houseboat right away. Brad, take his gun." Pop handed off my gun then grabbed me up as if I weighed nothing. Cradling me in his arms, he sprinted through the woods to the boat. I could hear Brad and Mr. Burnett puffing hard to keep up. Pop leaped onto the bow and struggled to the back, where he laid me out at his feet. The motor roared. A warm jacket was thrown over me from somewhere, although the warmth dissipated after a few moments. Unfortunately, my chill redoubled as the boat got underway in the frosty air.

Pop throttled the engine to full power and planed the boat out. I was aware of the fear on everyone's faces. Trees flew by in my vision. Pop kept shaking me with his free hand. The handle of the motor swung to and fro over my head as we skirted many obstacles. I slipped into a kind of warm stupor as time dragged on.

We had carried a bag of charcoal and lighter fluid for grilling that happened to still be in the boat. Brad and his dad emptied the contents of a couple of large coffee cans that we had been using for storage. The cans were converted to makeshift charcoal pots by filling them with charcoal and lighting them for heat. After the flames died down, they placed a pot between Pop's feet and huddled up to the one at their own feet. At least that's what I assumed from their hunched shapes. Snow was coming down harder now.

"Boys, y'all better stop huddling up and keep an eye out for stumps. I can hardly see through my glasses as it is."

It registered with me that we were at last skimming down Pack's Flats. It wouldn't be long before we'd be back. Without warning, the boat lurched upward in an agony of ripping metal and stopped dead in the water. Pop tumbled over me. The forms of both Mr. Burnett and Brad had disappeared from my view. Water ran beneath my back, rising quickly. The back of the boat was going down. Pop scrambled around, grabbed me up again.

"Git to the front of the boat NOW!" Pop shoved me against the other two, then threw himself on top. We all watched as the motor sank below the surface, then it gradually rose back up. The transom was just barely above the waterline.

I was pinned down, though able to witness the six-gallon gas tank floating away to the length of its fuel line and a pair of camo gloves drifting off. Dully, I realized that we had hit what henceforth would be called Death Stump. For now, it just didn't matter. I was too cold to care.

"Dick," said Vernon with solemnity, "we've gotta get him back to the houseboat fast, or we –"

"Dammit, Vee Bee. I know. Let me think." Pop gripped his hood, face scrunched in an agony of indecision. He searched around as if looking for another boat, his mass turning this way and that. "Vernon, you and Brad are gonna have to take those charcoal cans and use them to bail out the boat. Let me trade places with you so my weight will help keep the backend from going under while you work. Just make sure to take it real slow and don't go back there too far, or we'll sink for sure."

I was buffeted by legs and arms. Pop finally got settled on the very edge of the bow, holding me steady between his knees. I watched as Brad and Mr. Burnett sprawled out across the middle bench, trying not to add weight to the back of the boat. It appeared that the transom was maybe an inch out of the water. We weren't sunk yet.

With rapid movements, each of them filled the coffee cans and dumped the water over their respective sides of the boat. Each time one would lean out to empty, the boat would rock to that side and threaten to let water back in. Gradually the transom rose further and further. After what seemed like an hour, Pop was able to ease his way back to the motor and dipped some more. His hands were surely frozen. His face and the tops of his ears were almost purple. Mr. Burnett and Brad got me settled in between the two of them on the middle bench.

"Hold on, Ricky," Mr. Burnett mumbled in my ear. He was holding my shoulder. Brad remained still and quiet. I sat there and shivered.

At last, Pop pulled the gas tank to the edge of the transom and lifted it back into the boat. Although there was still a significant amount of water in the boat, he started the engine. Both Vernon and Brad looked at each other in relief. I couldn't understand how the motor would start either after having sunk below the surface, but it did. In front of me, just under the bow seat, was a wide crack just above the waterline. A tooth of cypress pressed up through the gap like an unwanted guest. Even as I watched, a ripple spilled into the crack and ran between my feet.

"Okay boys, I'm gonna start the motor and try to get us off this stump. What you gotta do is shift your weight toward me to keep that crack above the waterline. This is gonna be tricky. Brad, maybe you oughta come back here next to me." Mr. Burnett hugged me at the shoulder while Brad finagled his way back beside Pop.

Once again, the motor whined. Pop put it in reverse, gently rocking his body from side to side. I saw the cypress tooth extract itself from the crack. He then set us into motion toward the trestle, the Leaning Tree, the Three Giants, the Hair Bear stump, the Long Pond…and everything else faded.

"Dick, we're back. There's the houseboat!" Brad's exclamation registered with me. The hope of getting warm again flooded through my senses. A childish question washed vaguely through my thoughts: why did Brad get to call my dad by his first name while I had to call his dad Mr. Burnett?

"Me an' Brad'll git going on the heater and then I'll come an' help you with Rick. Brad, tie us off an' git duh door open!"

"Yes, Daddy."

They launched into the houseboat and fumbled around noisily for a few minutes. Then, "We've got it goin', Dick!" cried Brad.

Hands grabbed me from all directions. I was motivated inside, stripped completely of my clothes. Towels, rough like sandpaper, were applied to dry my skin. Embarrassment filtered through me as fresh clothes found their way onto my skinny, bluish-white body. I was still shaking uncontrollably, even in the radiant warmth of the large propane heater.

Vintage gas heater

"Let's stuff him into his sleeping bag," said Pop. He lifted me up while Mr. Burnett and Brad held the mouth of my bag open. He slid me right in with seemingly little effort. I was trussed up and pressed into a chair directly in front of the heater. Pop held my fingers nearer the glowing asbestos waffles. Bluish flames leaped between the bricks. It was mesmerizing to watch. That was all I could manage.

With the front door closed, the temperature inside rose quickly. As warmth permeated my joints, a new sort of pain attacked me.

"P-Pop? It f-f-feels like I-I'm b-b-burning."

"That's good, Boy. That means you're warming back up. Your body is telling you that you're going to be okay." His eyes were moist. "Just think. Without a bit of pain, life would be boring. You're alive, Boy."

Pop and Brad went back out to unload the boat and stow all the hunting gear. I sat by the heater, basking in its warmth. Concerned faces turned to relief and finally to relaxation.

Mr. Burnett bustled around in the kitchen area, heating water in a coffee pot. Unexpectedly, he turned to press a cup of hot chocolate into my hands.

"Thanks, Mr. Burnett."

"Harumph, you earned it, Ricky. By the way, you can call me Vernon or Vee Bee if you want." He looked me square in the eye as he said it. Something inside me soared over being given permission to call an adult by his first name. Things were beginning to look up around here.

Birds were plucked on the porch, followed by cleaning, followed by feeding the catfish with the remains. All the while, I stayed next to the heater. I didn't leave my spot, as every time the front door opened, cold air would spill in to send a shivering remembrance of what had happened earlier. I wasn't ready for any more chills just then.

Later that afternoon, pots and pans rattled as Vernon created a hearty wood duck stew (see Appendix for recipe). Any remnants of the early morning chill were vanquished as I spooned savory chunks of wild duck meat, potatoes, carrots, and brown gravy into my mouth. Filled with warmth, I once again sat back to enjoy the easy banter of good friends.

"Thank you, Mr., ah, Vernon, for the excellent meal," I ventured. I looked at Pop for his reaction.

"Don't look at me, Boy. You know the rule."

"I told Ricky it would be okay to call me by my first name, Dick. He's been through a real trial today. And it really ain't the first time, either. None of these huntin' trips are for little babies. I'd say he's grown into the right, wouldn't you?"

My cheeks grew hot, and my chest swelled. I could barely take a breath. Was this pride?

Pop rested his chin on his breast, then smiled. "I'd say so, Vee Bee, as long as the boy understands that he still has to respect his elders."

From that day forward, preparation for a Santee trip went to higher levels. Pop was determined that nothing like what happened to me would ever be repeated. But if it had, the story would have been much less dramatic as we were forever after prepared for the worst. I kept my mouth shut about the event after we returned home, having grown to understand the reason for the Santee Rule. Mommies would not take it very well if they knew the full stories about our hunting experiences. It is a good thing one cannot predict what comes next, as indeed, life was never boring on a trip to Santee.

"Who bravely dares must sometimes risk a fall."
~ *Tobias G. Smollett*

Barrel Hunters

It was circa nineteen seventy-four. Vernon, Pop, and I were exploring an area called Riser's Dead Lake above Sparkleberry Swamp. It was early fall, and the temperature was a comfy fifty degrees. A slight breeze puffed the Spanish moss around in the treetops here and there. The *Swamp Yacht*, the new, catchy name for our boat, droned along. I was wedged in my favorite spot near the front, legs propped on the bow, boat cushions at my back and bottom, with a bored expression on my mid-teen face. It was a look designed to needle my father if he chanced to tear himself away from his best friend long enough to notice. The name for the area seemed entirely appropriate as nothing remotely interesting was happening. Dead.

The men were downing beer and talking amongst themselves of higher things than I was privy to understanding at that point in my life. For instance, Mr. Burnett's oldest daughter's impending marriage was weighing on his mind, and apparently his pocketbook. He was not a rich man, so a wedding would take a toll on his finances. So would the speeding tickets that Brad was racking up on the weekends while traveling between the University of South Carolina in Columbia and home to wash clothes. I tried to imagine what over a hundred miles an hour on backcountry roads at night would feel like – tried but failed. My brain couldn't seem to generate the energy.

It was then that we slipped into a beautiful cypress-studded trail. The trees were tall and stately as if they had missed the harvesting at the start of the Santee-Cooper Navigation and Hydroelectric Project some forty years back. To build the hydroelectric dam meant harnessing both the Santee and Cooper rivers. Over one hundred seventy-seven thousand acres of swamplands and forests were cleared in economic and cultural progress names.

Directly in our path was the most enormous stump I had ever seen. It reminded me of tales about the size of trees in the Redwood Forest. In much the same condition as if the trunk had been lopped off last month, the behemoth was smoothly cut. Cypress didn't rot quickly.

Pop called out, "Boy, grab hold of that stump." He cut the engine.

I dutifully shifted to the bench, hung over the side with outstretched arms, and caught hold of a knobby protrusion as we coasted by. Deftly tying off to the stump with the bow rope, I studied the diameter in wonder. So did the men.

"Vee Bee, have you ever seen a stump that big?"

"Naw, Dick. That's a regular curiosity. You, me, and Rick could lay out comfortably on that thing without hanging off the edge."

"Hell, Vee Bee, that stump's as big as a flatbed wrecker! Tell ya what, this is as good a place as any to have lunch. Boy, git the sandwiches and stuff outta the cooler."

"Yes, sir." The moment food was mentioned, it seemed as if I was starving again. Gladly I started handing out the delectable fare. There's nothing like Vienna sausages, a whole sour pickle, a seven-inch diameter chocolate-drenched Chattanooga Bakery MoonPie, and an ice-cold twelve-ounce Pepsi in a glass bottle to make you feel good in the outdoors. While I munched, I gazed in wonder at the small spot of paradise we had discovered.

Directly after our respite, we attempted to measure the diameter of the stump by stretching our arms. It was hard to do since we had to lean out over the edge of the boat. We failed to reach around, but at least no one got dunked. So, we tried to count the tree rings instead. After surpassing four hundred, we lost track.

Vernon intoned, "Dick, have you ever seen such a hall of giants?"

"Nope, Vee Bee. It's truly amazing. Let's call it that – the Hall of Giants. Boy, untie us. We gotta go, or we might not find our way to the river before dark." Pop always knew how to engage me.

I removed the rope. The motor was pulled back to life. Everyone was comfortably full of fatty foods and sugary drinks, and we were off again up this fantastic trail.

Within a few minutes, I spied yet another wonder. This time it wasn't a stump but something way up in a tree along our port side. "What's that, Pop?" I pointed at the dark metal object some sixty feet high.

"Would ya look at that, Vee Bee? Is that what I think it is?"

"Shore is Dick. It's a rusty barrel. How'd it git way up there?"

"Beats me, Vee Bee." Pop pulled his camo cap off and scratched his head. "This is what hunters do down here. They make duck blinds out of steel drums, carry 'um up, strap 'um in the trees, and climb on in. Nobody at Ducks Unlimited is gonna believe this."

"Hey, look," I had been scanning ahead, "there's two more on up that way!" All traces of boredom had left me. This discovery took precedence over adolescent mannerisms.

Vernon said, "Dey get up dare and shoot down at dem ducks. There'll be ducks everywhere. Then they git another boat to come and find all dem ducks and pick up dem hunters after the shoot."

Marveling, Pop said, "This is duck hunting at its best – Santee style. You got to grip that tree like a squirrel, Vee Bee. A man would have to use his toenails and fingernails to go up there and shoot them ducks."

"Shoot down at dem ducks," chimed Vernon in awe.

"Vernon," Pop said with solemnity, "we'll have to bring a camera next time so we can get a picture of this. Who would believe people would get up in one of them barrels to shoot ducks?" He pulled the starter cord, and we were off up the creek again.

I was mulling over what a wondrous day we were having when up on the left came another remarkable sight. Speech would not come from my mouth, so I simply pointed.

This time Pop changed direction to follow my finger. He and Mr. Burnett were both astounded. In the middle of this wilderness of waterways, stumps, brambles, pigweed, and cypress trees was a one-story clapboard farmhouse sitting on a piled-rock foundation. The boat glided to the muddy bank. Despite the threat of squishy mud, we all climbed out to see this enigma.

The house was styled as if from the nineteen twenties. It sported a tin roof, a rock chimney on the right, a front porch with spindle posts, and horizontal siding. The siding had once been white but was now layered with mold and mildew. The front door was ajar. It was as if the owner planned to return shortly, but there was no one around. In fact, we had not seen another soul all day.

Pop trudged up to the front step. "Let's check it out." Gently placing a foot on the old boards, testing for strength, he stuck his head inside the door and let out a whistle.

"Whatcha see, Dick?" Vernon trundled past me to step up on the porch himself.

"We've got a regular house here, Vee Bee. Everything looks solid. It's not clean, but it looks safe enough. It hasn't been used in years. I'm goin' in."

"Careful, Dick." Vernon looked up at me. "Rick, mebbe you ought to stay out here just in case."

"Yeah, Boy. Hold whatcha got and keep an eye out. We'll be back in a minute."

I listened attentively as the men explored the interior of the abandoned home, imagination building tension in me all the while. Every shadow amongst the surrounding wilderness, every sigh of a breeze through the moss, every creak of boards from the men's weight led me to new conceptions of the situation. That included ghosts, wild animals, and other dark creatures.

I nearly bolted for the *Swamp Yacht* when Pop yelled from inside, "Come on in, Boy. All's good." Chills climbed my spine, but I steeled myself and entered the house.

Once inside, it became evident to me that the building was quite dilapidated. The pea-green paint was peeling from the plaster walls; every surface was covered in layers of grime. Left of the door perched an old refrigerator with rounded corners and a chrome handle. A porcelain sink was mounted to the wall under a tiny window that might have looked out into the side yard if it hadn't been so clouded with grime. Crouching against the wall opposite the refrigerator was a rusty gas range. In between was a rickety wooden table with three matching chairs. The structure had been retrofitted for electricity at some point using conduit pipe mounted to the walls between switches and fixtures.

Looking to my right, I saw a den of sorts. It held a couple of dilapidated upholstered chairs around a low wooden table. There was no sign of a television or other entertainment. The large window that looked out toward the swamp was coated in filth to the point that only a finger's width of sunlight filtered into the room.

"AAHHHHHAAAaaaaaahahhhaaaa!"

The sound erupted from the small door off the kitchen. My knees turned to water. Although I wanted to run, I could barely turn my head to stare in horror at the whiteish face leering out of the semi-dark doorway.

Vernon clamped his large paw on my shoulder and shook me. "Rick, it's okay. It's just me. Hey, Ricky!" He was chuckling.

The terror subsided. I pushed my glasses back up my nose. They had tried to slip off in the sudden sweat that was trickling from my face. I tried to smile but only managed, "G-good...one."

Pop spoke from deeper within the house. "Hey, y'all, come here and take a look at this."

"Come on, Rick. Let's go see."

I managed a few wobbly steps that gained in strength as I followed Vernon's receding form. I didn't want to be left alone. It turned out that there were two bedrooms off the hall. Rotten linens covered rusty iron bed frames in both. The end of the hall sported a bathroom of sorts. I could see a toilet. It seemed like an afterthought, or perhaps the water closet was nothing more than a roofed-over outhouse. There was no tub or shower, only a potty and a sink lurking somewhere beneath the grunge.

"Vee Bee, you know what I think? I think these people moved

out in a hurry because the water started rising when the dam was built. I'll bet they didn't want to give up their home."

"Mebbe you're right, Dick. As poor as people were back then, they surely would've took all the furniture and stuff."

To my surprise, Pop strode into one of the rooms and sat on the edge of the bed. It held his weight.

"Know what? We could use this place – like a hunting lodge. Spend the night next time, maybe. This would cut an hour off our ride to the hidey-hole."

"You think we can find it again, Dick? I mean, it was hard to see through the undergrowth."

"Sure, Vee Bee. When we get back to the boat, I'll mark it on the map. We'll check it out again before Thanksgiving. Bring sleeping bags and all. We'll call this our Rimini Hilton!"

"Heh, heh, heh."

"Come on, Vee Bee. We've still got a long way to go this afternoon. If you ain't moving forward, you're going backward."

I pulled up my sleeve to look at my watch. We had only been in the house for fifteen minutes. It had felt like hours. Gratefully, I left the Rimini Hilton. Little did I know that the very next trip to Santee would include a night in this abandoned domicile.

Pop said, "You did well in there, Boy. Nothing like a little bit of excitement to make life worth living!"

"You think dogs will not be in Heaven? I tell you,
they will be there long before any of us."
~ Robert Lewis Stevenson

Duck Dog

Just before my ninth birthday, Pop brought home a ten-week-old male Labrador retriever puppy. He was a squirmy bundle of energy with sleek black hair, huge, webbed paws, and floppy ears too big to be allowed. It was love at first sight. I suppose that's why I got the speech.

"Now look here, Boy. This dog is a hunting dog. I'll be training him to fetch birds for me. I'll let you play with him as long as you understand that you must not teach him anything that goes against his training. For instance, you won't be throwing balls or sticks for him to fetch. Instead, I'm going to use bird dummies only. You won't be teaching him stupid stuff either, like how to roll over and play dead or shake hands. He'll be taught to come, sit, stay, heel, lay, and bring back the ducks. Understood?" Pop had apparently noticed the disappointment that gripped me, for next, he said, "Now, now. I didn't say you couldn't play with him at all. I'll show you what you can and can't do. Tell you what, you can name him. How's that?"

That perked me up a bit. "Yes, sir."

What Pop didn't understand was the bond that grew between boy and dog was sturdier than the respectful acceptance that developed between man and dog. Sure, I followed the rules of engagement set down so I wouldn't spoil Pop's hunting dog, but Wolf became my constant companion from the first.

"Why did you name him Wolf?" asked Pop. "He's black as soot, and he's supposed to be a *duck* dog!" Exasperation played across my father's easy-to-read features.

"You said I could name him," I replied with a shrug. I had just finished reading Call of the Wild by Jack London. In fact, I had been devouring every frontier adventure book I could get my hands on. Besides, having a wolf at my side was *cool*. So, what if I wanted to be a cross between Daniel Boone and Superman when I grew up? Wolf was my dog, and he didn't seem to mind. He and I grew up together as real nature lovers.

Playtime with Wolf was really a training session for bird hunting. In addition to my usual reading, I found books on dog training methods for hunters, dog etiquette, and veterinary information for keeping hunting dogs in top physical shape. While Pop did the primary training, I reinforced and augmented Wolf's education. Every single day, after completing my homework, rain or shine, I was outside with Wolf practicing for hunting season. It was child's play.

Some say dogs can learn ten or twelve primary commands and perhaps another one-hundred-fifty or so random words. That may be true for some dogs, but Wolf was an exception from the start. He grasped all the verbal commands related to obedience training, all the hand signals accompanying them, and every directional order for finding downed birds under all types of outdoor conditions. From land to water, Wolf grew into a master hunting dog. I grew into his master. He would do anything for me and condescended to work for Pop.

In nineteen-seventy-two, when I was twelve and Wolf was three, Spartanburg experienced one of the largest snowfalls in its recorded history – seventeen inches. We lived in a quiet subdivision with a paved road sporting a half-mile-long slope nearby. For those in the northern states, be aware that we rarely ever have snowfall in the South, much less an event that sticks to the roads and is worthy of dragging sleds out of attics. This was only the second time I had ever seen snow.

Schools were out for over two weeks. Sleds that had been handed down through generations hit the big hill. Although Wolf could not join me on the sled, he ran alongside me as I rode all the way down. The slide was exhilarating, but the walk back to the hilltop dragging the sled, not so much. It was then that the sled dogs from Call of the Wild sprang to mind again. My sled was equipped with a loop of hemp rope specifically for dragging. I placed the cord in Wolf's mouth and told him to *heel*. His nose lined up with my knee as it was supposed to, and he kept pace as we climbed.

Halfway up, I grew tired, so I sat down on the sled and commanded, "Wolf, go home!" I really didn't believe Wolf would try to obey, but to my amazement, he did. Weighing out at nearly one hundred pounds of young muscle, Wolf not only pulled me and my hundred and twenty pounds the remainder of the way to the top of the hill, but he never broke stride. After that feat, I couldn't wait to find out what else he could be taught to do. Pop didn't need to know so long as Wolf behaved on the hunting trips.

The following year, we moved out to the country on twenty-three acres with woods, fields, and a stream. Wolf learned to wear my old army backpack loaded with tools and picnic lunches. We would make forays into the "wilderness." With so much space to work, Pop and I also trained Wolf in silent hand signals.

Nothing is more incredible to see than a trained hunting dog following silent commands to *sit, stay, lay, come,* and *go*. Wolf would also follow directional pointers to find and fetch up to six "birds," one after the other, each deliberately hidden from view by distance, foliage, and water. Wolf rarely lost a dummy or a downed bird. He never tried to eat the kill. His mouth never mauled a fowl. He rarely disobeyed a command, and only then if he were hungry or tired. In short, Wolf was one of the smartest dogs I've ever known.

Up until I turned sixteen, Wolf accompanied us on hunting trips. I enjoyed watching him work. His hearing, so much better than ours, made him a tremendous early warning sensor. He would turn his head toward the sound of ducks on the wing, or swimming ducks, or ducks preparing to land. Nervous excitement would course through him as he sat vigilant in the *Swamp Yacht* or blind, expecting ducks to go down when a gun came up. He remained poised to leap into icy waters on a moment's notice for retrieval of downed game.

One day in mid-summer, I had just let Wolf out of the kennel for his daily romp and training session when the neighbor came running up the drive.

"If you've got your dog out, Ricky, I would find him right away. There's a female in heat running around the neighborhood," warned Mr. Richmond. His bald head was pouring sweat.

"Thanks, Mr. Richmond," I said. The short man jogged up the road to warn the next neighbor as I ran to our deck to ring the farm bell. I was no good at loud whistling like Pop, but Wolf knew to come when the bell rang. For fifteen minutes, I swung that big bell to and fro – but no Wolf.

After a half-hour of walking the property and calling Wolf's name as loudly as possible, I was nearly unable to speak from hoarseness. Pop pulled in from work and joined me in the search. We drove around the area – still no Wolf.

Two weeks of sleepless nights and worried days followed. I searched everywhere in our rural neighborhood. Since I was no good at whistling, I used a sport's whistle in between my yells. Then, on a Thursday evening, March 18, 1976, exactly four months before my sixteenth birthday, I was ringing the farm bell desperately for Wolf when I heard a squeal of rubber come from the direction of the nearby highway. It wasn't five minutes later when our blue Chevy station wagon came roaring up the gravel driveway. Pop bounded out, waving his arms.

"Ricky, go get your mother and sister and tell them to get in the car quick! I've got Wolf in the back. We've got to take him to the vet right now!"

I ran into the house, told them what Pop had said, and then ran back to the car as fast as possible. While my mother and sister were making their way out the door, Pop had opened the tailgate. I climbed in with Wolf. Pop had laid him on the floorboard on a bath towel. Blood ran from his nose, and tiny whimpers of pain escaped

Duck Tale

from his lips as he tried to nuzzle my ankle. His intelligent brown eyes were clouded with fear. I stroked his floppy ear.

Pop drove us to the nearest veterinary clinic at high speed. I knew deep down that Wolf was in serious condition. I helped Pop lift him from the vehicle using the towel as a stretcher. We rushed him directly into the doctor's operating room. Then Pop directed me to go sit in the waiting area. After half an hour of the worst imaginings I had ever experienced to that point, Pop came out and told me the bad news.

"Son. Wolf has a broken pelvis. The doctor says that even with surgery, it is unlikely he will ever be able to walk again."

As brave as I tried to be, I couldn't see much through the moisture in my eyes. I simply nodded my understanding.

Pop heaved a sigh. "Wolf is your dog, so this is your decision. I will pay for the surgery if that's what you want. It will be expensive. Before you decide, I want you to consider a few things. First, Wolf is an animal. Animals are not the same as human beings. They don't live as long." He paused to let that sink in. "Second, Wolf is past middle age in dog years – and *was* an active hunting dog. He loved running down those ducks and bringing them back. Even with the surgery, he'll never be able to have fun doing that again." I tried to look into Pop's face but couldn't. He continued once more, "Think what it will be like if Wolf can no longer run and play and hunt those ducks with us. If he survives the surgery and heals, Wolf will live in pain for the rest of his life, whether from the surgery itself or from the inability to be the dog he once was. I'm going to give you a little time now to decide what you want to do. I know that it is going to be tough – a *man's* decision. I'll be back shortly."

My mother and sister were there too, but I barely noticed anybody else in those final moments as I held my best friend's muzzle.

The shot was given, quick and silent. One last lick on my palm and Wolf was gone.

A hand came down on my shoulder. "Wolf's in Heaven now, Son. I know this decision was painful for you. Just think how he's up there hunting ducks with the Lord. One day you'll get to see him again. I'm proud of you for letting him go so he can play, pain-free, forever."

Wolf has been gone from my life for more than forty years, yet I often think of him. Now and again, I'll have another good cry over his loss. Somehow, I don't think it really matters that he was just a dog.

He was *my* dog.

"Nothing makes one feel so strong as a call for help."
~ George MacDonald

10

One Good Turn

Everyone goes through pain, whether mental or physical. It's part of life. Pop used to say that God allows pain so people will look to Him for guidance and support. In his final two years, I watched Pop suffer unimaginable pain. During his ordeal with leukemia, his faith only increased.

Why is pain such a central part of life? Without daily pain of some sort, we tend to take things for granted. For instance, when this tale began back in the first chapter, one could sit out on Pack's Flats at midnight and see zillions of stars in the Milky Way. Now, because there's a huge waste disposal plant on the end of the Upper Lake, with massive lighting surrounding it at night, the stars are far more difficult to discern. It is this destruction of minor pleasures like stargazing that keeps many environmentalists complaining and protesting. It saddens me to recall what I used to see out in the middle of the flats at midnight. Of course, things always change, but not necessarily for the better. Perhaps that is why we age out and die, so the pain of remembrance doesn't overtake us as "progress" eliminates the possibility of repeating treasured experiences.

During the last half-century, I have witnessed a pristine wilderness become trashed by hunters, fishers, and the encroaching communities now building up along the banks. Trash thrown from boats, debris washed down the river, waste plastered in the trees to mark temporary cuts and trails – the volume increases yearly.

Both Pop and I were Boy Scouts, and when we grew older, scout leaders. Today this bastion of morality has been destroyed by the Politically Correct agenda. Fifty years ago, boys learned to be morally guided men. We were taught to pack out our trash, leave a campsite better than we found it, and help little old ladies across the street. Thus, Pop and I would remove debris from the swamp. Sometimes this conscientiousness would cause problems.

One frigid night Pop and I had just gotten back from checking the catfish lines along our fishing run. As we had traveled the run, we also removed ribbons of toilet paper that someone had draped over limbs along the way. Someone had used the material to mark a temporary trail up through the deeper part of the swamp, probably leading to a duck haven. We were comfortably settled on the porch, stargazing, discussing cosmic questions, when a far-off banging interrupted our deliberations. The sound was followed up with a barely discernable word, "Hhhheeeellllpppp!!!!" The echo passed on by us down through the swamp like a ghost speaking from the grave.

I turned to Pop, "What was that?"

"That's somebody lost in the swamp, probably." He snickered.

"Why's that funny?"

"Well," Pop reared back and stretched, "I've gotten lost up in there before with Vernon, and we had to spend the night in the boat. We weren't in danger – just lost until the sun came up."

I supposed that other people's pain could be humorous, but then the whine of a motor starting up way off caught my attention. The drone seemed to be going deeper into the swamp. "Looks like they're underway again."

"They're headed the wrong way," Pop said. I knew that too. My sense of direction in the wilderness has always been excellent. They were heading into the deepest part of the swamp, an area choked with stumps, pigweed, thickets, sandbars, and little open water in which to run a boat.

A few moments later, the motor cut off, and a rhythmic banging started up. Apparently, they were using their paddles as drumsticks against their boat. "Heeeeelllppp! Heeeeelllppp...." This went on for another half hour. The motor would start, run a little while, stop, then the banging and yelling would begin again. We could tell they were circling around somewhere up past Long Pond, near Catfish Creek, if you entered using one of the old cuts. Most of those sloughs were clotted with pigweed, brambles, and stumps, unnavigable when the water was low, like now.

Pop observed, "They must be a couple of zip-in-for-the-hunt tenderfeet that took too long after sunset to head back for the landing." Folks like these were commonly found ruining the hunt for real duck people. They zoomed out from the landing, sat on top of one's carefully laid decoys, utilized the expert duck calling from one's companions, and whizzed back out of the swamp at the first sign of sunset – usually just as the birds were flying.

Santee can be quite daunting at night. Every cypress tree, knee and all, looks the same. So does every island of pigweed, every marked or unmarked trail, every stump, and log. Even the shadows caused by modern navigation LED floodlights changed by the very moment, rendering clear pathways into unrecognizable courses to nowhere. That's why experienced swamp rats learn to look for landmarks like the Three Giants, the Leaning Tree, Hair Bear Stump, Death Stump, the Trestle, and many other navigation aids. Too, we always carried a trusty compass and a trail map. These poor lost souls apparently did not.

Just past midnight, we heard the distant motor die for the last time. By the splutter-splut-splut, it was plain it had run out of fuel. Two hours had passed since we first heard the noise; it had been our hope that they would find their own way out.

"Okay, I guess that's it then," said Pop, "We'll have to go get 'em."

"Why didn't we go find them earlier?"

"You know how far it is back to the landing. It'll take half the night to drag them out of the swamp. You want to go hunting in the morning, right? Up at 4:00 a.m.?"

I had to admit that staying up late when one had to get up way early did not appeal. "Why don't we just give them some gas and point them in the right direction?"

"That's what I intend to do."

About then, a shotgun blast rolled down through the swamp. It sounded like it was a mile away.

"Why would they be shooting this late?"

"They're scared, Boy. Tired. Cold. Out of gas. Lost. Wouldn't you try to get some attention that way? Why don't you load up your shotgun and shoot too? That'll let 'em know we're on the way. Be-

Map and Compass

The Global Positioning System for public use had not come into play during the '60s and '70s. We learned how to navigate using maps and compasses. I've always found it safer to have a working knowledge of where I am headed and where I have been without having to rely on a cell phone or other navigation device, especially in a swampland. Electronics aren't as reliable as old-fashioned knowledge drawn from years of experience. They tend to lose satellite connections in the swampy remoteness, provide inaccurate directions due to the everchanging waterscape, go dead at inconvenient times, get dropped in the water, or simply break. It's hard to juggle devices along with all the other hunting gear without something giving way. I recommend learning to truly navigate and not to follow instructions from gizmos proven to be unreliable in remote locations.

sides, Jesus said, 'Do unto others as you would have them do unto you.' You never know when you might be in a bad way and need help."

"Yes, sir." I did, and sure enough, they fired off another round in response. Pop jerked the motor to life, and off we went in search of the wayward boaters. Up the swamp through the familiar ponds, cuts marked trails we went. Pop would stop the boat every so often, and we would beat our paddles against the side. The lost hunters responded in kind. Eventually, we meandered our way through the tight cuts until the big halogen spotlight I held lit on a tiny jon boat. A couple of bedraggled young men sporting pale, bearded faces were shielding their eyes from the glare. I could see they were in quite a state. Their hunting clothes were thin compared to ours. Their boat contained no cooler with drinks. All they had was a couple of shotguns, spent shell casings scattered around on the seats and bottom, waning flashlights, and a tiny red gas tank that must be empty. Gratefulness radiated from them like the coming sunrise.

"How long you boys been out here?" asked Pop.

The driver said, "It's been hours – since last noon. We came to hunt for the evening shoot and got lost heading back. It got dark on us."

"You get any ducks?"

Mr. Blackbeard at the motor said, "Not a one. All this trouble, and we didn't even get a shot."

"Y'all ever hunted this area before?"

"No, sir," said the other fellow, Mr. Brown Beard. "We hoped to get a few ducks and make some stew after we got back. We're staying in a hotel down in Manning.

"That's quite a drive for an evening hunt. You boys hungry?"

They looked at each other and back at us, Mr. Blackbeard answering. "Yes, sir. Famished. We haven't eaten since lunch." Mr. Brown Beard licked his lips.

Duck Tale

"That was over twelve hours ago by my watch. Rick, how about pulling out a couple of packs of cheese crackers and Pepsi's for these boys?" This announcement brought smiles all around.

"I take it y'all ran out of gas?"

"We did, sir." Mr. Blackbeard mumbled, head hanging in shame.

"I assume your motor takes fifty-to-one ratio, gas to oil, right?" Heads nodded affirmatively. "Okay then, hand over that tank of yours, and I'll pour some for you. You got any fresh batteries for those flashlights?" Pop uncapped our six-gallon metal tank and tipped about a gallon into theirs. The smell of gasoline filled the air as fuel slopped out over his hands and both tanks.

Mr. Brown Beard said, "I've got one more flashlight here that's still working good."

Pop entered what I like to call his Command Presence. "Alright. Now here's what we're gonna do. There's enough gas here to get you back to the landing. We're going to start up the boats, and you boys are going to follow us to the main channel down by the trestle. You'll be able to follow the trestle right on back to Pack's. Just don't get too close to the pylons, and you'll be alright."

"Yes, sir," said Mr. Brown Beard, "All we have to do is follow the trestle. Check."

"That's right, and you'll be able to see the big mercury light on the point marking the entrance to the cove that funnels you to the landing. Just keep the trestle on your right and head for the light. It's only about a mile from here. Now, some advice. You should always keep a compass and a map in your boat. Boy Scout or not, you should live by the Scout Motto, 'Be Prepared' and the Scout Slogan, 'Do a good turn daily.' We're doing our good turn right now for you. I expect you to pay it forward. Is that understood, boys?"

Both spoke, "Yes, sir. We will. Thanks much for coming to help us. Thanks for the gas and for the food."

After that, it was purely a matter of leading the fellows out past

Hair Bear stump, the Three Giants, the Leaning Tree, and down to the trestle. They waved as they headed toward the now visible lights of the landing, relief awash on both faces. There was a puzzled expression mixed in, too, probably because they noticed we turned back into the swamp. I could just imagine what must have been running around in their heads. "Where are they staying up in there? Are they sleeping in their boat? How can they keep from getting lost in the swamp? They must be hardcore swamp rats. At least they were good people who were willing to help others in trouble. We were fortunate not to spend the night in the swamp without food, water, proper clothes, gas, batteries, map, compass, or experience. Thanks to those strange folks, we lived to tell the tale."

It may sound like overkill the way I described it. Still, there is always danger for those who come unprepared, especially if a watery wilderness is involved. Even folks with lots of experience sometimes get in a bind; hence, the admonition to do a good turn for someone else. Yes, several times, the situation was reversed for us, and assistance was most appreciated. Usually, it was motor trouble.

"Do not anticipate trouble, or worry about what may never happen."
~ Benjamin Franklin

Deserves Another

"Whing, ding, ding, ding," went the Evinrude, for the umpteenth thousandth time already this morning.

"Dammit!" erupted Pop, for the umpteen thousandth time too.

"What now?" He had been hanging out over the motor casing for several minutes with his hunting knife, cutting away cords of pigweed from the prop. Sweat streamed down his cheeks as he eyeballed the foot of the motor. "Another broken cotter key!"

Some days it was just unlucky to be navigating stump-infested waters.

Pop dropped back to his seat. "Boy, I'm out of spare keys. We'll just have to wait here till Alva and Vee Bee catch up to us. We'll have to borrow one off of them. I hope." The temperature was already climbing into the low seventies, so he stripped his jacket and rolled up his shirt sleeves. "How about handing me the canteen?"

I reached into the cooler for his army surplus jug of water and passed it over. He took a couple of swigs then handed it back. We needed no words. Besides, my teenage moodiness clamped my mouth shut. I was getting frustrated too. Here we were on a perfect morning in the middle of my favorite part of the swamp, and I couldn't merely enjoy the pleasantness of our surroundings. No, not, nada. So far, this was the third time the cotter key had gotten busted since we left the houseboat.

Earlier, I threw out the name Catfish Creek. That's where we were. It wasn't all that far from the houseboat. Catfish Creek twists far up into some of the remotest, pristine areas of Santee. In times

Typical Cotter Key
A cotter key is a strip of metal bent double like a hairpin. It is used to connect two separate parts together by inserting through holes drilled between them. Outboard motor transmissions used them between the driveshaft and propeller. Cotter keys are purposely designed to shear in case of extreme impact, so the two parts will hopefully separate without major damage.

past, there's no question in my mind the Swamp Fox himself holed up in there with his Patriots when playing hide 'n seek with British Commander Tarlton.

While we waited for the other boat to arrive, Pop and I surveyed the crystal water right down to the black bottom. Stately cypress trees, knees jutting from the water, shimmered in drapes of majestic Spanish moss. Verdant pigweed lined the edges of the trail. Stripers (striped bass) by the hundreds were migrating downstream about five feet deep, two-by-two, as if heading for the Ark. Clumps of large mud turtles sunned on every log. Dragonflies bigger than my hand flitted past ebony water snakes, some poisonous, draped lazily on low-lying limbs. These creatures were all around. We left them alone; they left us alone.

The buzz of the other outboard could now be heard, growing steadily. Resentment welled as I realized I would be taking a backseat to the camaraderie between the men again. It had been that way all weekend. "Rick, do this. Boy, do that."

Pop and the water moccasin

"Here they come, Boy. Stand up and wave them on over. I'm busy back here."

"It's about time," I muttered, "I mean...time they got here." I stood up and waved my arms.

"Look, Turkey, you've got to learn you can't control everything. I can't do a damn thing about motor problems. It's all part of the game. You just have to learn to make the best of things; otherwise, you're gonna be miserable the rest of your life."

"Don't call me Turkey!"

Pop's eyes blazed through his thick glasses. "If you act like one, you are one. Now straighten up, Turkey!"

I clamped my mouth shut, but it was touch and go. I was beginning to discover how painful it can be having to bite down on that vortex of rising anger instead of letting it out. It continued to smolder in my chest.

Shortly, a sleek new flatbottomed boat, as yet un-dinged by stumps, skimmed over.

"What the hell 're you doing, Meehan?" yelled Dr. Alva Pack, Pop's newest buddy. "We've been all up in the swamp looking for ducks, and here you are playing around. I told you we'd find 'em sitting on their asses doing nothing, didn't I, Vernon?"

"Heh, heh. Yeah. Whatever you say, Alva. Heh, harumph. Dick, you got a problem there?"

"Sure do, Vee Bee. Damn cotter key snapped again. Me and Rick won't be going anywhere unless Alva's got one in his ditty box."

"Meehan, Meehan! You know to carry spares around here. You're supposed to be the Mighty Duck Hunter, not some whiny-ass greenhorn." Our name is pronounced *Me-an*, two syllables, long *e* and short *a* with a silent *h*. Many people seemed to find it more fun to exaggerate our name as Meehan, long *e* and *a* and heavy *h*.

Pop told me that the enunciation didn't matter so long as people remembered who it belonged to.

"Lookie here, Pack Rat. Just paddle on over and say that to my face. Better yet, just paddle on over and gimme one so we can get underway. Time's a-wasting!"

Meanwhile, Vernon had been flutter-paddling their boat up to us. He had already retrieved Dr. Pack's tool kit and was jockeying the tongue of their boat so it would slide up under our raised prop to serve as a working platform. I had to admit it was smarter than hanging over the motor and trying to work with tools and tiny parts right over the water. Without a word, he unscrewed our prop to replace the broken key while I held the front of their boat to the back of ours as best I could while wedged between Pop's bulk and the side of the boat. What a production!

"At least Vee Bee's not being mean to me today," Pop said, slugging his thigh into my side. "He knows better than to aggravate me while I'm trying to find the greatest duck hidey-hole yet."

Turtles, turtles, everywhere
Photo courtesy of Michael Free, 2018

Dr. Pack crowed, "Just listen to that, Vernon. Even as we rescue his sorry ass, he thinks he can find a better duck spot than us. Meehan, I'll have you know that me and Vernon have already seen more ducks this morning than you'll see the rest of this weekend."

Pop said, "You just wait till this evening. Me and Rick'll set up the decoys and show you some ducks. Won't we, Rick?"

"Sure, Pop." I didn't put much enthusiasm into my answer.

Dr. Pack said, "Ricky knows the truth."

Mr. Burnett mumbled something that sounded like, "Ricky knows to get the work done first so we can play later. Harrumph.

Rumph." I smiled into his sky-blue eyes. To everyone else, he added, "Okay. Looks like everything's ready to go again." We pushed the two boats away from each other.

"It's about time," said Pop. "You can hardly find a good mechanic these days!" With that parting shot, he fired up our engine, and I took my seat. Finally, we were underway again.

The two boats took separate but parallel courses up the creek. Periodically, I could see Dr. Pack and Mr. Burnett through the trees, the good doctor driving with one hand and swinging the other freely while he bantered. Mr. Burnett crouched on the middle bench, chuckling, looking back over his shoulder now and again. He periodically shook his head as if in disbelief at some oddity the doctor must have said. They seemed to be having fun, and trying to imagine what outrageous things they were saying to each other began to douse the flame in my chest. The mood of the day was starting to lighten up until the boat lurched unexpectedly in the middle of the cut where no stump should be.

I could tell that we were gliding over something large. Glancing down, I saw what it was and immediately swung around to Pop. "Watch out. It's the hull of an upside-down boat!" At that moment, the motor flew out of the water with the usual ring-ding-ding and cut out.

Pop yelled to the other boat. "HEY, COME OVER HERE." He stood up and motioned to get their attention. They changed tack and headed over to us.

"What 'cha got, Dick?" asked Vernon.

Dr. Pack said, "Meehan doesn't know, Vernon. That's why he called in the experts." I could see his animated features hiding behind the latest wire-rimmed sportsman's glasses with the photosensitive lens that automatically darkened in sunlight and cleared up in the shade. Dr. Pack was a good salesman because we all wore them.

"Hush up, boys. Listen." Pop cocked his head to the side, pretending to strain. "I hear something up ahead."

We listened.

Sure enough, we all caught the distinct words, "I could use a hand if y'all don't mind." They drifted down from above. We looked up.

Prone across a limb was a bedraggled teenager with stringy black hair. His eyes were red-rimmed as if he had been up all night, or perhaps boozing, or both. I laid my claim to the latter. We were momentarily stunned.

"What 'chu doin' up there?" Pop was the first to recover. "Is this your boat sunk here?"

A moan issued from the lanky frame. The teen had no shirt, only nasty, torn blue jeans and muddy sneakers. Filth covered him.

"I say, boy, are you hurt?"

"Naw, sir. Not really."

Pop kept talking, "So, what happened here?"

"My...my friends...we ran out of beer, see. So, I was elected to go back to the landing and git some more. I guess I got lost."

Dr. Pack said, "I think you got more than just lost." To Pop, "Dick, I don't think even all four of us could get his boat turned back over, do you?"

Pop thought for a moment, then he said, "Let's give it a try. Vernon, maneuver your boat over on this side of the hull, and Rick and I'll try to lever it up your way using our paddles. Now, Rick, I don't want our paddles broke, so don't force it too much. Take it easy, got it?"

"Yes, sir." I handed a paddle back to him and took hold of mine. Applying pressure as directed, the two of us only managed to shift the sunken hull toward the other boat.

"Stop, Ricky." Pop looked up at the teenager. "Alva's right. We aren't going to be able to turn your boat back over. Maybe if we get you some more help, someone can figure a way. What do you think, Vee Bee, Alva, do we split up and go find a lake warden, maybe? And what do we do with *him?*" The last was said with a thumb pointing up in the tree.

"Well, Dick, if we split up, maybe we can get him some help without wasting too much of our day," said Dr. Pack.

Vernon grunted his agreement, rather unenthusiastically it seemed to me. My sentiments ran the same way. Reconsidering, I realized it was one of those times when people could die from a wrong decision. I begrudged the loss of time spent in a rescue effort but didn't want anyone to suffer and perhaps die.

The teenager's wane voice drifted down, "W-what about my friends on up in thar? We got anuther boat. If'n y'all don't mind too much, maybe I could climb down and git in with one of you 'uns and lead you to 'em?"

"How long you been up there, anyway?" asked Dr. Pack.

"Since last evening."

"You mean you've been hanging from that limb all night?" Vernon was a study of amazement. "Hell, man, you must be numb. Harumph, bubbsa."

"Ah is."

"Well, climb on down here and get in our boat then," said Dr. Pack. "Meehan, I say we let him lead us to his friends if he can. Hopefully, they'll be able to take care of him themselves."

The teen was shakily making his way down the cypress trunk. He slipped and fell, splashing us all. Vernon and Dr. Pack reached down, grabbed him under the arms, and flopped him into their boat like we do the giant catfish. He was pale, thin, and shivering.

Dr. Pack handed him a spare jacket from his boat trunk. "What's your name, son?"

"I's Enus – Enus, ah, Talbert."

"Well, Enus. This is Vernon, and I'm Alva. That's Rick and Dick over there. What'd y'all do last night, anyway?"

"Oh, a little of this, a little of that."

"I figured as much. You were doing some drugs too." Dr. Pack was looking at the youth's eyes. "Yeah. Drinking and drugs, Dick."

Pop said, "Okie Dokie. Let's find his friends and make sure they're okay. Lead on, Pack Rat. Time's a-wasting."

Mr. Burnett propped Enus on the bench beside him, gripping the youth's arm so he wouldn't fall back out of the boat. Enus pointed on up Catfish Creek. So much for enjoying the ride.

We worked our way northerly for the next hour or so, following the license plate markers as usual. The beauty of our surroundings contrasted against the negativity in my mind concerning our new ward. Enus, without support, would definitely have fallen from the boat. I wondered what kind of drugs would cause that. After all, he and I were about the same age – fourteen-ish – and the school had taught me to "say *no* to drugs," maybe not cigarettes, which tended to be "like father, like son," but to leave drugs alone. Some great public service announcements on television warned against abusing drugs, alcohol, cigarettes, starting forest fires, and littering. It was obvious this guy had not paid heed to them. He was a mess, and even more so when I saw him wretch over the side of the boat, most of the vomit cascading down his bare arm.

I couldn't hear what Dr. Pack and Mr. Burnett were saying. I supposed they were making the best of the situation by their animated motions, probably discussing side trails that promised some decent duck spots. The eye doc preferred to appear laid back, down to earth, but behind his spectacles, there was a quick, analytical mind. While the motor droned, I pondered why these three very different men could become such fast friends. What did they have in common? It took many more years to learn that friendship is forged through hard work, just like anything else worthwhile. I turned to ask Pop what views he held on the subject. As usual, he put into words an answer I could understand.

"To make a friend, you must close one eye. To keep a friend, you must close both." Over the years, I have come to recognize this as an axiom. Not wishing to plagiarize, I did a bit of research on this phrase to see who may have coined it in the past. There are several variations out there, but only one that might have predated Pop's usage. Author Norman Douglas, in his book, London Street Games, published in 1931, was the phrase, "To find a friend one must close one eye – to keep him, two." The book is in the public domain.

I looked at Enus's thin, pale back and pondered whether his friends would be of any help or if they were in as bad a shape as he. I got my answer in a skinny minute, as out of the gloom ahead emerged a floating cubical with a full porch. It appeared to be at least twice, if not three times, the size of our houseboat. It was big. We were awed.

Mr. Burnett and Dr. Pack erupted. "Would you look at *that*! Can you believe anyone could build *that* all the way up in here?"

Pop and I glided up to them. I grabbed the gunnel of their boat to keep us all together.

Enus perked up and wailed, "Tommy, Andie – where y'all at?"

From within the houseboat came a slurred, "Zzzzaat yew, Enus. Where you been all night? Me and Andie, we thought you was dayud." Then, nothing more.

It took a moment for my eyes to adjust so they could penetrate past the open door into the dimness within. What I saw both amazed and horrified me. A rather plump, well endowed, naked as a jaybird form was hanging droopily over what appeared to be a full-sized bed. At first, I thought I was looking at a flabby arm, but then I realized it was a heavy breast. My cheeks grew hot. I had never seen a naked girl before. Shaking off the initial shock, further scrutiny proved that Andie had been beaten with the proverbial Ugly Stick. However, that didn't seem to matter to these boys. After all, looks are only skin deep. What's underneath is all that counts, right? I kept telling myself that as a shaggy head rose above her rounded shoulders to peer at us. A modicum of shame must have made this new male person throw the sheet over Andie as he struggled to rise.

As wiry of stature as his friend Enus, Tommy, every bit as pale, and every bit as wasted, wobbled over to prop against the doorframe, wearing nothing but his birthday suit. I averted my gaze from his privates.

Pop fired off, "Boy! Go put some clothes on. We don't need to see your shriveled little whang!" To the rest of us, he said, "Now we know what these boys have been doing. I think we've seen quite enough. Vee Bee – toss that boy up on the porch there, and let's go."

"Er, Dick? Don't ya think we oughta make sure they can git back to the landing? Harrumph." Vernon peered over his wire-rims, skeptical.

Dr. Pack said, "Yeah, Dick. Vernon's right. We can't leave 'em here till we know they're at least somewhat sober. Hey Tommy, y'all got any coffee in there?"

"Yeah, I think so." Tommy reappeared in filthy underwear, the likes of which I'd never seen. "Come on in and make yersef at home."

To my disbelief, we all piled out on the porch, where I rooted myself. Dr. Pack went inside and got their percolator going. Shortly the aroma of very stout coffee wafted out the door.

The Big Boys took hold of the situation. Before long, they had all three of those inebriated youths on their way to recovery, pumped full of black java. And yes, there was more retching.

Meanwhile, to keep the teenagers talking. The adults kept firing off questions.

"How long did it take you to build this damn thing all the way up in here?" asked Dr. Pack.

"What were y'all thinkin' taking drugs and drinkin' brown liquor?" asked Vernon.

"You can't mean that you carried all this lumber and material by boat and built this contraption on the spot?" asked Pop.

The answers were a bit incoherent at first, but they became stronger as the morning moved into the early afternoon. Slowly the tale unfolded. Apparently, the teens lived in nearby Pinewood, South Carolina, a tiny, rural town. Both boy's families owned boats for fishing at Santee. The youths had spent the better part of a year hauling building materials all the way up the Creek, so to speak. Erecting the facility had been a massive undertaking. The boys had learned good carpentry skills over the weekends and summer vacations from their fathers, home builders. I understood this, as I worked for my father the same way.

Long story short, they had ready access to scrap wood, tools, and knowhow – about too many worldly things. Although this *megastrosity* of theirs was one of the best homemade houseboats I had seen to date, its sole purpose was debauchery.

Andie, the so-called girl, was Enus's good friend from school. She also seemed somewhat dimwitted, with veiled eyes, greasy black hair, and other parts I prefer not to describe again. Let's just say that she was along for the ride.

"Vee Bee, Pack Rat, Rick. I guess that about wraps up the mystery. I think these boys have learned a hard lesson for one weekend. I take it that you boys will be able to make it back to the landing?" The question was kind of left hanging.

"Uh…I think we'll be okay," murmured Tommy. Enus only nodded. Andie had nodded off.

"It's time to go," Pop said. "Before we do, though, there's just one more thing I'd like to mention, boys. Now, we don't mind helping people in real need, see? It's just that we don't have a lot of time on the weekends to waste helping fools and their whores. I suggest y'all spend a bit of time getting straightened out before you ruin your lives. I'll bet Alva and Vernon here will agree with me that sending along a lake warden to check on you this afternoon would be the right thing to do. I'd hate for the three of you to die way out here because of teenage stupidity!"

It amazed me to see how those words lit a fire under their butts. As we piled back in our own boats to leave, there was a hurricane of activity from the teens inside. I suspect drugs and other illicit materials were either being packed away or destroyed. All I know is we were leisurely making our way back down Catfish Creek when we were passed by the trio. They were still mostly naked and didn't look at us. Instead, Tommy goosed their engine until their little boat was planed out amid all those trees and stumps. It was a marvel they escaped the clutches of the swamp without sinking another boat. The last we saw of them, ever, was Andie's wide, white ass bouncing on the bench.

Every so often, Pop and I would return to see the Mega-strocity at the end of Catfish Creek. It seemed that no one ever came back to use it again. After a couple of years, it melted into the muck of its own accord – swallowed by the Santee as if it never existed. Mold to mold; mildew to mildew.

"Never trouble trouble till trouble trouble's you."
~ Anonymous

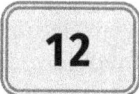

Toy

We were heading down through the backcountry of South Carolina on a two-lane highway, traveling fifty-five miles an hour, the new speed limit imposed by President Nixon to conserve fuel on a national level. Pop and Mr. Burnett were sitting up front fuming about it.

"I'm telling you, Vee Bee, those Arabs in control OPEC (Organization of Petroleum Exporting Countries) are pissed off at us for supporting the Israelis against 'em."

"I don't know, Dick. All I'm sayin' is the price o' gas has jumped from thirty-eight cents to over fifty-five cents a gallon in just the last couple of weeks! That's a forty percent jump, an' it's killin' us, I tell ya! People won't be able to afford to put gas in their cars before long."

"What ought to be scaring you, Vee Bee, is the way the stock market is dropping because of all this garbage. That's going to really hurt people in the pocketbook. Next will be increasing prices at the grocery store, you know, inflation. We could put a stop to it all if we increased our own petroleum production. I think it's a crying shame that we're dependent on a bunch of Arabs for our fuel when we've got plenty of oil in our own country!"

Mr. Burnett was shaking his head as if in disgust. "If them pansies in Washington would get outta the way and let our refineries get at it, we could break that OPEC embargo and get back to seventy on the highways!"

We were out in the middle of nowhere at four in the morning, going to hunt ducks. All the politics was putting me to sleep, especially since I didn't understand much of what they were saying. Wolf, black as the surrounding night, was lolling among the waders and such in the back of the Toy. Through bleary eyes, I saw an old four-door sedan ease out from a roadside gas station onto the highway, directly in our path.

"DICK, LOOK OUT!" Vernon gripped the dashboard, bracing himself for impact.

I saw Pop twist the steering wheel to avoid the collision. The Toyota Land Cruiser jolted onto the dirt shoulder of the road, passenger side. I could see a steep embankment below us. Glancing back, I noticed the other vehicle had stopped in the middle of the highway. All this occurred inside a split second.

The Toy bounced up onto the pavement once more. It seemed we would right ourselves and be okay until the steering wheel was wrenched out of Pop's control. The vehicle launched sideways into a roll down the center of the highway. Curling into a ball, I watched the headlamp spin past at least six times. Meanwhile, I remained weightless in midair. I could almost have twiddled my thumbs.

Pop's right arm shot back to grab me. I couldn't believe how he contorted like that.

He missed.

I saw Wolf being tossed among all the gear as if in a clothes dryer.

The Toy spun off the road's left side into an open field where the terrible noise stopped abruptly. I landed on all fours in the middle of my bench seat, unscathed.

Vernon was groaning and holding his nose, blood running freely down his chest. He turned the rearview mirror to look at the damage. There was a deep gash in the bridge. It sickened me to see it.

Wolf was licking my face and neck.

Pop grimaced as he turned to me, "Are you hurt?"

"No sir."

He grimaced again and turned back around to face the steering wheel. I noticed the wheel was cocked up at an odd angle. I also discovered that the whole roof of the vehicle was shaped like the letter V.

"Boy, I need you to walk back up to that gas station and get them to call an ambulance. Take Wolf with you. Make sure the driver of that other car doesn't leave. We need her insurance and contact information for the police. Call them too. Vernon, you okay?"

"Nose hurts. Everything else seems okay, Dick." His words were mumbled and slurred. No, he wasn't at all okay.

I gratefully exited the car. Wolf didn't have to be called to come. He exited right on my heels. Pop handed me his wallet through the nonexistent driver's window. The orange-and-white Toy looked as if a giant child had stepped on it sideways and set it up right again to admire his handiwork.

I followed the swath of churned dirt back to the highway. We had rolled several hundred feet, making it a trek back to the filling station. The attendant was full of concern. A small black woman, the other driver, was on the telephone at the cash register with the 911 emergency operator. I marveled over this, although the system was a few years old now. I had never witnessed anyone using 911 before. To be able to dial that simple number for help was simply amazing. She reported the accident and called for an ambulance. Tears streaked her cheeks as she watched me. I could tell she was terrified.

"Everybody's okay, ma'am," I said. "My dad and our friend will need a little patching up, but nothing too bad." Relief gushed from her countenance at my words. I turned to the station attendant. "My dad asked for a bottle of aspirin."

"Here ya go. Take it. No charge." He was a young man with straight brown hair hanging to his shoulders. He pushed the bottle of Bayer across the counter. "Glad y'all are okay."

When I got back to the Toy, Pop and Vernon had exited. Wolf circled the vehicle as if to ensure nothing else was going to attack us. Vernon held a bloody strip of cloth, torn from his own undershirt, across the gash on his nose. His glasses were in his other hand, two pieces separated cleanly at the bridge.

"Let me have that bottle, Boy." Pop quickly unscrewed the metal cap and emptied at least ten tablets into his mouth. He swallowed them all at once, dry. While we awaited the ambulance, I couldn't help noticing that Pop would wince every time he took a step. "Vernon, you gonna need an ambulance ride too?" That question scared me.

"No, Dick. I'll get cleaned up when I git back to the house. Roberta's a good nurse. Mine's not as bad as it looks. I think my own glasses cut me when my face hit the ceiling. I'm gonna walk up there and give her a call."

It seemed like the ambulance and police took forever to arrive. I could hear multiple sirens in the distance. Pop sat down and propped himself against the front tire on the driver's side to await the arrival. Vernon had gone up to the store.

The policeman was an amicable fellow, stalwart, honest face. With his gun belt, he was most intimidating. Pop had to answer questions while sitting in the cop's car. The black lady did too. I felt sorry for her. When all that was done, the medics from the ambulance forced Pop onto a stretcher.

"My boy's riding with me. Hang on a second. I need to talk to my buddy. Hey, Vernon?"

Vernon sluggishly walked up to the stretcher. "Yeah, Dick." One of the two orderlies stepped up to him to get a look at the gash on his nose. "I don't need nothing, thanks."

"Vernon, I'm taking Rick along with me. Do you have a ride?"

"Yeah, Roberta and Brad are on the way. They'll be here to git me within the hour. Is there anything you want me to do for you?"

"Sure, Vee Bee. How about giving Ann a call and let her know what happened. Tell her I've got Rick, and the ambulance is going to take us to Spartanburg General Hospital." Pop was beginning to fade a bit. "And, if you don't mind, get the Toy towed into Clary Smith's garage on Country Club. I'll settle up with you later. Okay?"

"No problem, Dick. I'll come up there to see how you're gittin' along tomorrow. I hope everything checks out okay. Rick, take good care of your daddy. Hear?"

"Yes, sir."

Duck Tale

To make a long story short, Pop's back was broken in three places. He remained in traction at the hospital for several weeks. It took years for him to recover most of his mobility. To this day, I have no clue how he could stand after the accident in that condition. I also believe that he may have broken his own back trying to protect me. The way he twisted around, with his right arm grasping at me, was an unforgettable image. What does all this have to do with duck hunting and Santee, you ask? Let's chalk it up to the whole hunting experience. I was learning that pain teaches us things. Things like how to appreciate what we have. Things like counting your blessings. Things like how to be a man.

Man, it was one beautiful day. Pop was finally ready to get back out into the world after the car accident, so he went and found another vehicle. He bought a good old American-made Chevrolet Suburban two-ton SUV. It was built like a tank. He decked it out with gun racks, mud-grip tires, lots of emergency gear, and a CB (citizen band) radio, which was more fun on the highway. It worked like a walkie-talkie. Mash the corded handset to speak. Release to listen. Change the channel for different frequency bands for semi-private conversations with other travelers. It was mounted under the dash, and I was itching to fiddle with it.

"Breaker, break, break," said Pop into the handheld microphone. Static. "Breaker, I say breaker, this is call handle Ducky Blat One, license 0469er. "How's the traffic getting through the Capital of

Southern Hospitality (Columbia, S.C.), red tractor-trailer on the northbound run?"

More static, then, "This is Big Charlie O in the big red cab heading north. Come back?"

"Check, Big Charlie O, I repeat this is Ducky Blat One out of Sparkle City (Spartanburg) heading down to Santee for a weekend of fishing with my boy. What's the traffic like getting through Capital City? Come back?"

"Ten-four (acknowledged), Ducky Blat One. The traffic...static...static..., 10-4?"

"Come back, Big Charlie O, come back. Somebody walked all over you (talked over your transmission). Say again, 10-4?"

"Watch out for plain wrappers (unmarked police cars) at Newberry. No more smokies (cop cars) after that, so put the hammer down (speed up, no police). Have a great weekend! This is Big Charlie O, heading up the road in the Big Red Roller going 10-7 (signing off)."

"Preeshaydit (I appreciate the information). We saw a Kojak with a Kodak (police car with radar) at Marker 16. Be careful, Big Red Roller, and thanks for the intel. Ducky Blat One, out."

CB radios in cars, what would they think of next? I could hardly wait for the day Pop would let me give it a try. It was *cool*.

"Boy, we'll be down at Santee in no time. Hold onto your hat." The tire noise rose in pitch.

"Hey, Pop, do you think we'll catch any catfish this weekend?"

"We'll catch something, for sure."

"How's your back doing?" I wanted to spring it on him when he wasn't looking. Pop never complained. All those nights he was laid up in traction, looking like a marionette, told me that I never wanted to go there, not ever.

"Don't you worry. Your old daddy can still whip your tail. I'm doing fine."

Besides putting out catfish lines and sitting on the houseboat porch, we went sightseeing up toward Sparkleberry Landing, planning to cut over to Riser's Dead Lake and back out to the river in the afternoon. The spring weather was perfect, comfortable, pristine. The water was clear, the air temperature seventy degrees. Bugs had not yet made their presence known after a long winter. Snakes were still sluggish, even while sunning themselves on the low cypress branches. We had to make sure we didn't bump them out of the limbs with our heads as we slid underneath. Since it was hard to tell which ones were poisonous, we had to assume all were. As we progressed up the flats, I tried to imagine what I would do if a snake dropped in my lap. It was going to be an interesting day.

Showing a poisonous snake

We were skirting around the islands at the upper end of Pack's Flats when suddenly, a couple of Florida Everglades airboats came screaming up the flats at fifty miles an hour. Together they sounded like a twin-prop airplane, scaring up coots and all kinds of other critters. Pop turned off the motor so we could watch them. We marveled at how they thumbed their noses at stumps and logs while we were relegated to cautiously picking our way through the swamp.

"Boy, look at the way those boats don't draw hardly any water. They aren't even hitting any stumps!"

"They're going up into Sparkleberry like us. Let's follow them." I was fascinated with the strange boats.

Pop started us up, and we slunk in their general direction. We could hear the boats crisscrossing the flats on the other side of the islands but couldn't see them.

KERBLAM!

The explosion was so loud we both rubbernecked. There was smoke rising from behind one of the little islands. Pop immediately gunned the engine and adjusted our course. It was likely someone would need assistance.

When we banked around the closest island, a fantastic sight met our eyes. One airboat was up against the island's shore with a gigantic log thrust up through its safety cage. The wooden propeller was cropped off to a nub. Smoke was rising from the big engine behind the driver's seat. The driver himself appeared to be shaking his head as if to clear it.

Pop cut our motor, "Are you okay? Do you need help?"

The airboat driver turned to look at us. "I'm okay. Can't say my boat is. I radioed my partner already. He's on the way." I noticed headphones dangling around his neck.

A few minutes later, the other airboat came shrieking around the island. It was apparent they had their own problem under control, so Pop started us up again. For once, we didn't have to interrupt our day to help others. Perhaps these aren't sage words, but a carefree weekend is hard to come by. Sometimes it's nice not to be needed.

Fast forward to the fall of nineteen eighty-six. I've mentioned a couple of times that we would go out into the middle of Pack's Flats at midnight to watch the stars. This night was the last time the Three Duck-kateers and I were at Santee together in the same boat. I was twenty-six and still a gofer. The only difference was that the Duck-kateers now respected me as a married man. Not only did I fetch stuff, but I got to be the driver. I drove all the way down and back, and I got to drive the boat all weekend, designated, of course. I didn't mind in the least. I felt comfortable among my older, wiser, and dare I say it, equals.

"Would 'ja look at that. Can you believe the incredible beauty of such a transient thing?" The dark form of Alva was obviously in a neck-craning position.

The only lights anywhere around us were coming from the heavens unless you counted the lone pinpoint of the landing's mercury lamp over a mile away. The flats were like obsidian, reflecting the myriad of stars and one other incredible thing – Halley's Comet. On a clear night throughout the year, anyone could look up and see the approach of this historic ball of stellar debris. It was a minor spectacle for the naked eye, but even better with binoculars.

"Gimme those things so I can see too, bub brah, Alva," said Vernon. "You've been hoggin' 'em."

"I call them after you, Vee Bee," said Pop. "Rick, I can't believe you forgot to bring our own binoculars."

"You said that you would get them off the counter," I countered.

"Did you hear that, boys? Now that we treat him like a real man, he thinks he can sass his poor old daddy. You think I ought to backhand him?"

Vee Bee said, "We need him, Dick. He's the driver."

"I don't want to end up driving either, Dick. I'm on vacation. I think you should leave Ricky alone," Alva said. "He mixes my drinks just right too. Never screw with the bartender. He might spit in your cup."

Vernon chuckled.

"Mutiny, that's what this is." I could see Pop's shadow shaking its head. "The moment my boy finally becomes a real asset, everybody else wants to horn in. Boy, gimme another two-finger." Pop passed his cup over, and I dutifully used my index and middle finger horizontally to measure his portion of brown liquor. It was a heavy drink, about four ounces of alcohol. These Big Boys could sure play hard.

All that could be heard out there in the middle of the flats from that point were my dropping ice in cups, pouring drinks, the shifting of bodies in the boat, and far away splashes of unseen origins. All of that died away after I handed out the next round until only breathing could be heard. We all silently admired the comet, realizing it would probably be the once and only time in our lives that such an event would occur. It would be three-quarters of a century before Halley's made it around the Sun and back to Earth again. We were sitting there staring at entropy in a nutshell. I dredged up my schoolboy recollection of the Second Law of Thermodynamics.

Halley's Comet 1986
Public domain image from
https://www.nasa.gov/directorates/heo/scan/images/history/March1986.html.

"I wonder how much longer the comet will give off enough gas to be visible to the naked eye?"

"What do you mean?" asked Pop.

"Well, the mass of the comet is constantly burning away as it orbits around the Sun. I was taught that comets are a great example of how the Universe is winding down, burning itself out, sinking into chaos – the Second Law of Thermodynamics." I felt very cerebral.

"Hum."

"Hum, harrumph."

"Ahem. Looks like I got my money's worth."

"Er, brub, what'da ya mean, Dick?"

"You can't beat a Wofford College education."

Laughter rolled across the waters.

It was then that I noticed the shadow of another jon boat drifting by off to starboard, no lights, no motor, like us. A deep male voice sprang from the shadow, "You boys need to turn on your running lights before you cause an accident. I'll let you off the hook this time because it's such a beautiful night, but don't let me catch you out here doing this again." The other boat's lights came on, its motor roared, and the glassy smoothness became ripples of muddled reflections.

I started to fume at the rude interruption. Here we were out in the middle of nowhere, trying to enjoy a once-in-a-lifetime cosmic event, and still, the real world found a way to horn in.

Alva said, "I felt something burning my ass, didn't you, Vee Bee?"

"Something, er, harumph, yeah. I seem a little lighter too."

"I think we've all been winding down anyway. Boy, get us back to the houseboat before we fizzle out."

And so, my brainwave about thermodynamics went down in flames. All I can say is that sometimes the threat of trouble is worth the risk to achieve a shining moment of pleasure, sort of like not using a condom. I don't know about you, but I intend to see Halley's Comet come around again. Hey, I may be a hundred and two when it does, but I intend to make it in blazing glory if the Lord be willing and the creek don't rise.

"Love is a canvas furnished by Nature and embroidered by imagination."
~ *Voltaire*

| 13 |

One Starry Night

Like a one-armed bandit, the ancient gasoline pump at my shoulder clicked dollar tallies and gurgled up fuel. Meanwhile, in her seductive crescent guise, Luna undulated in the black waters of

Duck Tale

Pack's Flats. Was she flaunting her beauty? Erotic notions swayed through my fourteen-year-old head to the doo-wop refrain of Dootsie William's *Earth Angel* drifting over from the radio of Vernon's faded blue '51 Plymouth Coupe. Loose camouflaged pants, starry skies, and rhythmic sounds made discrete my current adolescent predicament.

"WHATCHA DOIN', BOY?" The Command Bellow plowed across the open water with such force that my ethereal connection snapped. My goddess left me jilted on the end of that rickety old wooden dock. "DON'T JUST STAND THERE. TURN OFF THE PUMP!"

How strangely apropos was Pop's comment.

"TURN IT OFF! TURN IT OFF!" Pop's voice turned frantic. I cat-walked down the narrow dock to comply, twisting the gasoline pump's on/off handle. The sound of gushing stopped abruptly.

For a moment, silence reigned, but only a moment.

"Y'all about done out there?" yelled old Mr. Joseph Britton Pack Sr. himself, through the screen door of his bait shop. "I wanna close up. I've been here all day. I'm tired, and I wanna go home."

Pop and Rick on the dock at Pack's Landing, 1974

"Don't get your panties in a wad. We're a-coming," said Pop. "Besides, you only have to walk thirty yards, and you'll be home!"

Vernon snickered.

"It ain't a matter of distance, Meehan. It's a matter of food. My wife's got me a good bowl of fresh catfish stew on the table, an' I wanna eat it while it's still hot!"

Pop rejoined, "Well, maybe you ought to invite us to supper then. We like catfish stew."

"Go git yer own! Now hurry up!"

To me, Pop said, "Come here, Rick. Take this money up to the cantankerous old cuss. Tell him we got $18.23 in gas. The total should be somewhere around $25.00 with launch fee and the bait." He raised his voice toward the screen door, "Tell Pack the price of gas here is highway robbery!"

The sound of someone blowing a raspberry from the direction of the bait shop wafted over to us as I took the money from Pop and headed over to pay out.

"Did you hear that, Vee Bee? Someone's farting up a storm around here."

"Yeah, Dick. An' the price o' gas *is* too high. Harrumph."

"Old Man Pack's gotta make some money somehow."

When I entered the shop to hand Mr. Pack the money, he was standing by the cash register, chuckling. "Yo daddy sure is a pistol. I'm gonna miss him when I retire. Grandson's gonna take over for me. You met Jody?"

"Yes, sir. Jody's a bit older than me. From what I heard, you send him out as a hired fishing and hunting guide. I also heard that he runs your commercial catfish lines now."

"He's a good boy. Taught him everything I know. He's all growed up. Could do anythang he wants, but he shore does love being here at Santee. He's got it figured upside-down an' back'erds. I'm proud of that boy for wanting to take after his grandaddy."

Mr. Pack handed me the change. I said, "Jody's got a good grandpa." Mr. Pack visibly puffed out his chest. Since I only saw him once a year or so, in a way it was like watching time-lapse photography of a person growing old. It saddened me to see it. My own paternal grandfather had recently died, and the memory was still too fresh. I clamped down hard on that reflection.

"I like yer daddy. He's a good'un too, I'm sure. Been coming here for years now. Y'all have a safe weekend an' I'll see ya Sunday. Hope you catch a bunch of cats. Tell Meehan that jus' cause I like him don't mean I ain't gonna charge him. In fact, I'll charge him double if he crosses me." Mr. Pack raised his craggy voice, "AND IF HE DON'T LIKE IT, HE CAN FIND ANUTHER LANDIN'!"

The words, "…ornery old cuss…" wafted through the door. Mr. Pack and I both laughed as I turned away. The friendly banter was typical when Pop interacted with others. My own attempts to be like that were worthless flops for the most part. Somewhere deep in my being, a hint of jealousy annoyed me.

With the usual foofaraw, the boat got stuffed and launched. Only the dark picket of moss-covered cypress surrounding the cove kept us company as we idled out of the no-wake zone and up along the trestle. I glanced back at the single mercury lamp hanging askew over Mr. Pack's bait shop door. The old man was locking up. I didn't know it was the last time I would ever see him. I turned back to scanning for stumps, the high-intensity floodlight at the ready as we slipped into the Vastness.

My earlier mood reasserted itself as I took in the beauty of the cosmic scene over the flats. We were angling toward the Leaning Tree, visible as a shadowy finger in the distance. Unbidden, the word *nevermore* rose to the forefront of my mind. Where did that word come from? Oh yeah, *The Raven*, by Mr. Morbid himself – Edgar Allan Poe. I had read the poem aloud in front of my English class last week. My agile fourteen-year-old brain churned out the opening line of the poem, "Once upon a midnight dreary, while I pondered, weak and weary, Over many a quaint and curious volume of forgotten lore –"

"Sure is gittin' cold out here," said Vernon over the engine drone. "Think we brought enough propane?"

"There'll be enough to burn down the houseboat."

"Oh ho, humph, eh heh heh." Vee Bee half-laughed, half-groused.

My face was beginning to freeze up, which made me long for Vernon's big propane heater after my past experiences with Santee in cold weather. I gave up trying to recapture my weighty meditations as my discomfort grew.

"Make a sharp left, Dick. Now right."

"I know, I know."

"Well, how come you missed the turn last time then?"

"Whaaaat? I know this swamp like the back of my hand."

"Where is it, then?" yelled Vernon. His tone caused me to spin around. Two ghostly faces wore concern. My guts knotted up as I realized they were talking about the houseboat.

"Could we have missed it again, Vee Bee?"

Vernon shook his head. "How? We've been here a hun'derd times! This is the way."

I jumped to my feet and swung the Big Light around our little hunk of metal. Our new illuminator was a homemade work of art, a car headlamp glued by polystyrene foam inside a round metal office trash can. Battery clips on a pigtail hooked it to a car battery. I was beaming a quarter-mile circle like I was a giant searchlight. What a miracle!

"Whoa, Boy. Slow down. We can't see a thing. You're blinding us." Pop sounded subdued somehow.

"Dick, let's back up an' see if we passed it." Pop somewhat hastily whipped us around. I nearly lost my footing and decided it would be best to sit back down. I held the beam grimly ahead.

"Here, gimme that light, Rick." Vernon took the bulky device from my hands.

"Hey, Vee Bee, bring it back to your left. Slowly, slowly." Leaping reflections in Pop's glasses heightened the feeling of surrealism creeping into my mind.

Where was the houseboat?

As the beam came back around to port, Pop barked, "Stop Vee Bee!" He cut the motor.

I adjusted my glasses. Then I squinted hard. What was I looking at? Two logs? No – pontoons. "There it is!" I yelped, immediately embarrassed by my outburst. I discovered both my arms pointing and quivering of their own accord.

"It's sunk!" Pop exclaimed.

"There ain't no way. . ." Vernon trailed off.

I went rigid as realization struck me. How could this have happened? I turned to search Pop's face for the truth.

"I'm telling you it's *sunk!*" The finality in Pop's voice rang like a death knell across the silent swampland. He started the motor. In moments we slid up beside our ruined houseboat. The pontoons appeared to be in fair condition, but the entire *house*-portion of the boat was missing.

Pop clicked on his flashlight and washed the rusty drums with its yellow beam. Vernon sucked in his breath. I saw it at the same instant. Pop's light had settled on the one-inch mooring cable, which was nearly hidden below the water level. It seemed to be squeezing the middle of the houseboat like a belt cinched too tightly.

The boat dipped dangerously close to the water as all three of us leaned over to follow the cable into the depths. It took both Vernon's and Pop's flashlights combined to see a few feet under the murky water. The cable dropped beyond the straining light, yet we all made out the side of our beloved houseboat – beneath us.

Pop standing on upside-down houseboat pontoon

"It's upside-down," I breathed.

"I think you're right, Boy." There was sadness in Pop's voice. Vernon remained silent.

Not ready to acknowledge the destruction of the houseboat, I looked around at the trees. Grey bark and strings of Spanish moss reflected our lights back at me. It was then that I noticed something strange. For as far as the light reached, the cypress trees parted like a *V* down through the swamp. I followed the odd wedge back across our houseboat and out the opposite direction.

"Pop?" I asked.

"Yeah, Son."

"What's wrong with the trees?" I swept my arm in an arc.

"Look, Vee Bee." Vernon turned the Big Light to follow Pop's pointing.

"What 'er y'all talkin' about, Dick?"

"The trees, Vee Bee, the *trees,*" said Pop. "It must have been a tornado. Look at the way they're all leaning."

Vernon peered owlishly around as he spoke. "Sure. A tornado could 'a come through here a couple 'a weeks ago when we had that bad storm up at home."

"Yeah. Talk about the Wrath of God. The only way the cable could 'a wrapped around the houseboat like that is if the whole thing got cut in half."

We looked at each other in silence, then back down at the old pontoons. Could it really have happened like that? Surely not. But here was the proof. The end of our hunting trips, all the fun, all the good times...

"Well, Vee Bee, at least you were right about one thing."

"What?"

"That cable."

"What do ya mean?"

"You said it would never break." Pop sighed. "If we ever build another one of these top-heavy mothers, remind me to figure a better way to tie it off."

Vernon hung his head, "Looks like our houseboat's done seen better days."

"We had some good times, didn't we, Vee Bee?"

After mustering a little courage, I asked, "What do we do now, Pop?"

He didn't answer immediately. I could tell Vernon was waiting to hear the answer too. All around us, the hush was palpable.

"We go home." There was no voice of Command in Pop's simple statement, only mixed awe and sadness. Luna winked down coldly while Santee reflected her fateful beauty.

"It is hard to fail, but it is worse never to have tried to succeed. In this life we get nothing save by effort."
~ *Theodore Roosevelt*

Resurrection

"It'll take a helicopter, I tell ya!" Vernon's voice clapped out over the whine of two outboard motors.

"Heave ho, Vee Bee. Heave ho!" I could tell from Pop's bearing that all was not well with the production. However, they were com-

Duck Tale

mitted and could not stop without risking damage to the boats and possibly themselves.

I was standing atop a huge cypress stump about forty feet from the action, barely above water level. My legs were cramping. The only relief I could get was to squat now and then. Although it was uncomfortable, at least I could see everything.

It was not pretty.

Two jon boats were hauling against blocks-and-tackle, lurching hither and yon, like wild animals trying to break their bonds. A huge cypress tree looked as if it would be ripped out of the swamp by the roots. Something was bound to give. Perhaps I shouldn't have told Pop earlier that it would be impossible to raise the houseboat, unlikely perhaps, but not impossible. He was now on a mission to prove it could be done.

Pop's latest quotable quote was still clanging in my skull as I watched this dangerous scene unfold. "Son, anything's possible if you want it bad enough!" Simple, ineloquent, but to the point. I had been pestering him about our sunken pleasure boat, wanting to know if we could build another. I kept at him for over a week, reminding him of all the good times yet to be had. So, here I was, tagging along for the Big Deal. Utterly useless. Literally *stumped*.

One of the things I heard discussed was how much weight in soggy plywood and fiberglass insulation would have to be pulled out of the water. Other questions arose, too, like how to apply forces great enough to flip the houseboat back onto its pontoons. A plan was formed, which hinged on the weather. Any effort to salvage the houseboat had to be soon. The longer the wooden structure remained sunk, the more waterlogged it would become. So, two weeks after the initial discovery of our lost happy spot, here I stood, hoping for success.

"Vee Bee – angle more to your right. NO! YOUR RIGHT!" Pop was definitely upset. The two boats swiped each other again.

Brad said, "Daddy, do you think we're gonna get it this time?"

"Aaah, oooh. Humph. Things ain't lookin' too good. Dick, we got to come up with a new plan."

"Okay, Vee Bee. Let's stop for some lunch and figure something out."

Pop brought the boat over to retrieve me while Vernon and Brad began unloading fare from their cooler. In all the excitement, I hadn't realized I was starving. We paddled back over to them and exchanged Pepsi-Colas for thick sandwiches of ham-and-cheese on rye.

I had no idea how to raise the houseboat, so I listened to my elders discussing it while I ate.

"Vee Bee, what we need to do is tie the block and tackle as high up in the tree as we can so we can get a better angle on the rope for lifting the roof off the bottom. Since your boat is smaller than mine, I think you should pull the tackle. I'll use my boat to pull the rope tied to the tree-side pontoon. Lift and twist at the same time, see? That should allow us to flip the houseboat over."

Vee Bee crossed his arms. "Sounds good to me, Dick. Brad here will shinny the tackle higher up the tree. Neither of us can do it."

"I can get it, Daddy," said Brad.

"Okay. Let's give it one more try. Rick, now that we know what we're dealing with, you'll stay in the boat with me. And Vee Bee, make sure to angle away from us when all the pulling starts."

"Heh, heh, yeah. We don't want to slam the boats together again."

Tying off everything according to plan took another two hours. It required some real doing to force a rope down under the water and get it threaded around the porch support at the roofline. After all, the roof was on the bottom of the swamp, about eight feet deep. Pop and Vernon both got soaked. Brad and I were mainly spectators, using our paddles to hold the boats in position as best we could until it came time to climb the tree and move the tackle up higher. Brad struggled mightily but was only able to shinny another six inches up the tree with the rope.

"Boy, gimme your bow and an arrow." Pop had me pack my Bear recurve bow, although it was a mystery why. While I strung my prized bow and drew a good, straight, wooden arrow from the quiver, he reached in the toolbox to get a roll of nylon twine. I reluctantly handed over my favorite weapon and watched him tie the string off near the arrow's fletching.

"Pop, *please* be careful with my bow."

"I'm not going to hurt your little bow." Pop stood up, drew my recurve back to the maximum (which made me cringe), aimed high in the air, and let the arrow fly. It shot up a good hundred feet before it dropped the string neatly over one of the highest branches in the nearest big cypress. The line played out as the arrow plunged down into the water.

"First time's a charm, Dick," said Vernon.

"What a lucky shot," said Brad.

"I don't mess around, Boys. Luck had nothing to do with it. It takes skill. Let's hoist up the tackle." Pop removed the arrow from the string, handed my bow and arrow back to me, and passed the end of the string to Vernon.

The free end of the big rope was then tied to the nylon string. Brad and Vernon pulled the string, drawing the heavier rope up and over that high branch. Shortly, the rope, now sporting a double block, was dangling from the high limb, the other end still tied off to the underwater porch support at the roof of the houseboat. All that was left to do was tie the rope's business end to Vernon's boat. The second attempt to raise the houseboat could then commence.

"That'll have to do, boys," said Pop. "Don't stop for nothing once we get this thing moving. If it comes out of the water, we've got to bring it over all the way, or it'll just sink again."

The boats got started. The lines got tugged as planned. Once the sheer weight of the soggy houseboat came into play, things got dicey. Both outboards protested as throttles were gunned. The bows of each boat angled sharply upward. I could not see ahead of us at all, but that didn't matter since we were fixated on watching the houseboat as it wobbled under the strain of forces threatening to rip it apart.

The big cypress creaked in protest as the roof slowly lifted out of the muddy water, audible over both revving motors. Water showered from the big rope as it sang like a plucked guitar string under the increasing tension. Pop gave it more gas, a turmoil of muddy wake spouting behind us. The far pontoon rose ponderously from the water.

"Give it all you got, Vee Bee!" Pop yelled above the noise. Both boats seemed to redouble their efforts. Water spilled over our transom, but Pop didn't slow down.

Gradually the far wall of the houseboat rolled over toward us. Fully three-quarters had risen from the mucky bottom. Water poured out of the front door. At our angle, I could see bedding and gear sloshing around inside. Another few moments and the houseboat's own weight would finish the job for us.

Then it happened.

The houseboat was floating on the pontoon that was now dipping deep under the water. Unfortunately, there was enough play in the ropes that the whole structure slipped toward us. In seconds, the houseboat sank again.

Successive attempts yielded no better results. It was only that one time we were even able to get the pontoons nearly flipped. The day was waning.

"We tried, Vee Bee."

"Harrumph. Well. Yeah. No joy, though. Looks like it's a goner, Dick." Vernon was detaching his block and tackle while Brad held their boat against the tree. I saw Vernon almost lose his balance and fall in. I also saw his hand fly out to the tree for support – and get punctured all the way through by a large rusty nail. Vernon's scream pierced the surrounding calm and froze my insides. With a mighty wrench, he pulled his hand free. Blood spurted everywhere, along with epithets the likes of which I had never heard from Vernon's mouth. I couldn't blame him.

Out came the *Swamp Yacht's* first aid kit. I held the boats together while Brad and Pop worked on Vernon's poor hand. I found it painful to watch his suffering. There were no words, no funny grimaces this time.

"Hand me that moonshine, Brad," said Pop. Brad reached into their cooler and extracted a small flask of Vernon's own home-brewed liquor. "Vee Bee, this is gonna hurt like a son of a bitch, so get ready." Like in the movies, Pop disinfected the wound with the alcohol in the liquor, working it into the puncture with his fingers. Even as I watched, Vernon's whole arm was swelling. Perspiration streamed down his reddened cheeks. A low moan issued continuously from between his clenched teeth.

"Daddy," said Brad, "I think we ought to get you to an emergency room."

Vernon mumbled, "I think you're right. Dick, me an' Brad will head into Sumter. I'll see you back in Spartanburg. Let's go, Brad. Humph, oomph."

"Yes, Daddy." Brad switched places with his dad. Their boat whipped around and out of sight in what Pop referred to as a *skinny minute*.

"Pop?"

"Yes, Son."

"I hate that Vernon got hurt like that."

"Me too."

"Is he going to be okay?"

"I sure hope so. His arm got swollen in an awfully big hurry. That worries me, Boy."

"Why, Pop?"

"Because that means some real bad infection from that rusty damn nail has gotten into his bloodstream. I've seen people lose arms and legs over that kind of stuff. Well, I'm sure he's going to be fine. Brad will get him into the hospital in an hour or so, and they'll fix him back up. I hate it for him, though. Brrrrrr....it reminds me of stepping on that board and ramming that nail through my foot last summer." He wiggled his ankle.

"I was standing there, Pop," I said, trying not to think about it. I had seen the nail come through the top of his right foot – only it had been a pristine, shiny nail. Not an ancient-swamp-water-rusted-dull-nail. Even that "clean" nail caused Pop a lot of anguish for weeks afterward. Antibiotics, soaking the foot, wrapping it in an Ace bandage, and using crutches to get around. Just thinking about watching him navigate the stairs at home still scared me.

"Pop, do you think we'll try again to raise the houseboat?"

He pierced me with his expressive eyes. "Not just no, but *hell* no! I think we've paid enough of a price today."

I supposed that sometimes the price for a little bit of pleasure was not worth it. Until now, I had never witnessed Pop give up on anything. Usually, he beat a problem until it squealed for mercy. This was the first time I had ever seen him beaten instead. Now I knew what it meant to see defeat written on someone's face. I bid a silent goodbye to the houseboat as we packed it in and headed for home. To my great disappointment, I had discovered that no one was infallible, not even Pop.

"Life affords no greater pleasure than that of surmounting difficulties, passing from one step of success to another, forming new wishes and seeing them gratified."
~ Samuel Johnson

15

The Redo

"Boy, building a houseboat's a whole lot of expense and trouble."

"But Pop, just think of all the good times we had." I could tell that

I was wearing him down, especially with my next quip, "We aren't getting any younger, you know."

"I think about it all the time. That's why I talked Vee Bee and Alva into partnering with us to build another one."

"Us?" I was in my last year of junior high school, 1975. Between Boy Scouts, playing the saxophone in the band, studying Biology, English, History, Mathematics, and other subjects – how could Pop think I would have time to help with the project?

"You betcha." He paused in cleaning his shotgun long enough to fix me with his Demand Glare. This differs from the Command Presence in that it means I'm going to have to suck it up, whatever *it* is. "This one you're gonna help build. You're old enough to learn what it really takes just to have a bit of fun. Besides, you'll appreciate it more if you're involved."

"But Pop, I'm so busy in school and stuff. When will I have the time?"

"Nights and weekends just like me. You wanted this. You got it. If you're not stepping forward, you're going backward. Besides, you might learn something."

Got it, I did, exactly as described. I began hiking the mile-and-a-half from Evans Junior High School every afternoon to Marko, Inc., our family's janitorial supply business. The business resided in an old brick building with a dank basement and a half-moon tin roof. Mommy worked there too, as a secretary. While at work, I had to call her Mother. I could look over into the YMCA field from the back loading dock. I used to play little league baseball there during the summers. After completing my homework in the salesmen's back office, after filing invoices or making copies on a thermal copy machine for Mother, after helping the warehouse personnel with loading and unloading truckloads of janitorial paper and supplies for inventory, after five o'clock when everyone else would go home, Pop and I would step out to the side yard to work on the new houseboat. Shortly after that, Dr. Pack and Mr. Burnett would arrive to help. Sometimes, Marko's warehouse manager and assistant would also cut metal, tighten bolts, bang nails, run wiring, and lay in a few pipes. The payment was made in beer, naturally.

Houseboat II was also built on the heavy trailer that would haul it to Santee. The difference in construction was vast compared to the original. Instead of a heavy wooden structure, this domicile was built atop an old pontoon boat platform, framed in one-inch angle iron, covered in aluminum siding, spray-styrene insulated, and the pontoons themselves again filled with floatation foam styrene too. It was apparent this design would be far lighter and more stable than the original from the start.

Sparing all the details, suffice it to say that this work rose to completion over a long, hot summer of nights and weekends. When school let out until the Fall, I discovered my actual capacity to withstand heavy labor and heat. I suppose you could describe it as learning to *do or die*. Since I had no intention of dying, that left only the *do* part. I learned to git 'er done.

Indeed, this major project was completed, launched, and placed in a permanent position near the old sunken houseboat, where it was moored for the next forty or so years. Many great weekends were spent aboard, like the one where Pop and I caught a bunch of breams.

"How y'all doin'?" Pop waved at the young couple canoeing by the back of the houseboat. It was early morning, and the sun was beginning to peek through the trees. Unfortunately, he was on the poop deck, the tiny back porch where we had painted a crescent moon over the backdoor. My great-grandmother once had a ? painted on her outhouse too, but hers was an enclosed structure. Thankfully, Pop wasn't hanging *it* over the side. He was sitting on the potty chair. I saw the woman avert her gaze and her man start to paddle faster. I felt embarrassed, but not Pop. He came back in smiling and raring to go.

"Didn't it bother you that those people saw you...ah...you know?"

"Nah, Boy. T'ain't nothing they ain't seen before. Let's go fishing."

We didn't start the motor since we planned to fish in the immediate area. The ripe smell of nesting bream had drifted over us continually since we arrived yesterday. The water was clear, black, six feet deep. Water lilies were blooming. It was a perfect Spring morning.

Pop raised the motor so we wouldn't get tangled. The gentle current allowed us to float down through the runs and cuts heading toward the trestle. The scents of various flowering plants coupled with earthy decay rode the gently moving air. We dropped our hooks loaded with nightcrawlers and sat back to watch our bobbers. As with all activities akin to this, we asserted our patience.

"Pop, how do you get girls to go out with you?"

"You ask them, Boy."

"You mean, you just walk right up and ask them?"

"Simple as that."

I pondered on that for a while. Little clouds of gnats were eddying around the clumps of pigweed here and there, the sun glinting off their tiny wings. Now and again, a bass would jump to grab at them. We weren't fishing for bass, though. Like bass fishing, girls, so far, had eluded me. I was probably just afraid to walk up and boldly talk to them like Pop was suggesting. I felt stupid.

"Hey, did I tell you what happened when I was down here with Alva and Vernon last month?"

"No, sir."

"You missed a real adventure. Vernon busted out a couple of teeth."

"How'd he do that, Pop?"

"Well, let me tell you, it wasn't easy. He had to work hard at it." Pop paused, probably for dramatic effect. It seemed to me he was building up a story that really didn't amount to much.

"Okay, Pop. Tell me." All thoughts of girls slipped away as the tale unfolded.

"We were getting packed up to come home. I was out on the boat getting the gear all arranged, weight distributed, all that. Vernon and Alva were inside tidying up. You know the last thing to do before we lock up?"

"Remove the hose from the propane tank and make sure there's plenty of fuel for the next trip. If not, bring the tank home for a fill."

"Right. So anyway, I could hear Alva cussing about the brass connector being so tight that he couldn't get it loose by hand. Vernon was telling him to move out of the way so he could get at it with a monkey wrench. Evidently, Vernon got down on his hands and knees and tried to untighten the nut holding the hose to the tank, and the wrench slipped and busted him in the mouth."

Once, I flubbed a catch, and the baseball split my lip against my front teeth. I cringed at the memory. "So, what happened then?" I couldn't stand not knowing. Call it being a glutton for punishment.

"I heard Vernon give a yelp, and then Alva called for me to bring the first aid kit and hurry inside to give him a hand. Vernon was propped against the table with his legs sprawled across the aisle when I got in there. Pack was hovering over him, shining a flashlight in his mouth. Blood soaked his shirt. Nearly scared the woolies off me."

Pop had to interrupt his story because I got a bite. "Hook him, Boy, hook him. You know we've gotta catch something for dinner tonight. Hunter's Rule #2."

I whipped the pole to set the hook in the fish's mouth as I had been taught. The bream fought hard, jerking the line back and forth for a few moments, then gave up the struggle as bream tend to do. I reeled in the pan-sized fish, removed him from the hook, dropped him in the pail Pop held ready, reset my hook, and placed it back in the water.

"Vernon was groaning and holding his hands over his mouth, so I reached in my duffle bag and got a clean towel. Alva said, 'Dick, Vernon's lost a couple of teeth. Busted them out with the wrench. I found one on the floor, but the other's hanging on by a thread.' Vernon took the towel from me. When he pushed it against his gum, the other tooth came out. I went back out to the boat, got the last of our ice from the cooler, helped Vernon wrap it in the towel, and watched him place it back on his gum."

"Wow. That must have really hurt," I cringed.

"Yeah, I'm sure it did. You know, teeth hurt when they first come out, but the pain subsides fast enough. Alva and I got him some aspirin and brought him home. The moral of the story is to be careful about removing that fitting. Once we got back, I was able to get my homeowner's insurance to send him a check to get his teeth fixed, five hundred dollars. I had almost forgotten that the houseboat was covered. You know what Vernon did with the money?"

"Got his teeth fixed, right?"

"No. Alva told me yesterday that Vernon was showing him his new Winchester Model 12 pump-action shotgun. They stopped making them in 1964. Vernon wanted one since he was a kid. Top-notch gun, he said. Told me they started making them in 1914. You know he's a gunsmith after hours to make a little pocket money. You've been in his shop. Vee Bee does love a good gun." Pop got a bite…but missed it.

"But what about his teeth, Pop? You mean he didn't get them fixed?"

"Nope. Probably won't either."

"Why not?"

"Teeth fixing is an expensive proposition."

Visions of trying to smile at girls without some of my front teeth sent shivers up my spine. It was hard enough just to say hello to one while dealing with my current liabilities. I had frizzy hair, four eyes, railroad track braces, and spindly appendages. Some things must be more important than personal comfort. I just couldn't imagine what.

After more than forty years, I found out. While fact-checking the stories herein described, Alva corroborated Pop's version of what happened to Vernon's teeth. A month later, I spoke with Brad for the same reason. I asked Brad if his father ever got his teeth repaired. Brad said he really didn't know, but he did remember getting a beautiful new Winchester Model 12 pump-action shotgun from his dad for Christmas.

"As soon as there is life there is danger."
~ Ralph Waldo Emerson

16

Various and Sundry

Perhaps the greatest lesson the Outdoors can teach is how to react appropriately to current circumstances. Like a baseball pitcher throwing an unexpected curveball, the wilderness tends to change suddenly in unanticipated ways. No one can predict what will happen in the next moment, so it is best to be prepared for anything.

"Hand me the spark plug puller, Son."

"Here ya go, Pop." The boat bobbed in Pack's Flats near the infamous Death Stump. We were drifting, the wind and current sending us toward the trestle. No other boat was in sight. It was a bright June midday, the warm sun making the water sparkle. Thousands of black-feathered coots were clumped together up and down the flats like teeming islands.

"Take this," Pop handed me the extracted spark plug. "Get a rag from the toolbox, pour some gas on it, and clean the plug while I scrape the duckmeat outta the intake ports." Duckmeat is the common name for *Spirodela polyrrhiza,* a tiny (1 mm) floating disk of a plant that infests Santee. From a distance, it looks like a green scum covering wide swatches of the swamp. The plant clogs the intake jets of outboard motors. This has caused our engine to overheat several times and once burned out our water pump. We had to beg for a tow back to the landing. We certainly didn't want that to happen again.

Pop had removed the motor cover to get at the spark plug, so now he sprawled, exposed flywheel on the motorhead to reach the ports. They were on either side of the shaft just above the prop. It was a stretch, even for him.

I cleaned the carbon buildup from the plug as best I could and handed it back. Pop replaced it, reconnected the cable, and prepared to try the motor again. A dozen pulls on the cord later, the engine sputtered, choked, coughed, and roared. Now that the motor had started, Pop did not slow down to replace the cover. It remained in the bottom of the boat at his feet as he steered us toward the Leaning Tree. I was just twisting my new swivel seat to aim forward when we hit a stump.

The motor flew into Pop's lap. He caught it by the flywheel, probably trying to prevent the chainsaw-like gear from grinding into his kneecap. Instead, the wheel cut a quarter-inch wide groove right down the lifeline on his right palm. He pushed the motor back into the water again with his left, then turned toward me with one of his funny grimaces. I nearly laughed, but then I saw the extent of the injury.

Pop's pain threshold always astounded me. Things that would have brought me to my knees in agony only caused him to moan and make funny faces. Pop opened his hand to inspect the injury, exposing what appeared to me to be either white bone or cartilage. I know the blood must have drained from my cheeks.

"It's okay, Son. Buck up. You're gonna have to work on me."

Here we go again. Another emergency with no one around to help. "Pop, don't you think we need to get you to a hospital so you can get that stitched up?"

"Nah. This ain't nothin' but a little ole scratch. Find me that bar of soap in the bottom of the toolbox and get out the first aid kit."

Now, I had been through multiple emergency response classes, from basic first aid to advanced lifesaving, at the YMCA and in the Boy Scouts. I had the certifications and merit badges to prove it. I knew better than to scrunch up my face and tell the victim how bad their wound looked, but I had to bite my lip this time.

Pop finished soaping and scrubbing the gash thoroughly with swamp water. He held out his hand to me, holding the wound open so I could use some of his brown liquor, whiskey, to disinfect it. My hands were shaking badly as I splashed the burning fluid into the wound.

"Ahhhhhh" was the only sound he made.

I then squeezed a whole tube of antibiotic ointment into the gap. Pop massaged his hand to thoroughly fill the groove with the cream. I applied multiple layers of cotton gauze to the wound, followed by an Ace bandage wrapping to keep everything in place and germ-free. It was a grizzly affair that caused me to wince and squint and have nightmares.

"Are you sure you don't need to go and get stitches, Pop?"

"You don't go to the doctor for every little thing, Boy!"

Pop traded places with me. I pulled the motor to life, and we went on down the lake. After all, we were there to find a new duck hidey-hole below the trestle. Pop toughed the weekend out. For the next few months, he kept stretching the hand to keep his mobility as it healed.

Pop and I returned to the houseboat. It was a good thing he hadn't hurt his left hand. If he had, he would have had to let me drive. He always got antsy when I had the tiller, perhaps because I wasn't yet an expert at skipping over logs and stumps. Peering through the trees, I could see that our friends Alva and Vernon were already back from checking the catfish hooks. They were parked on the porch, Alva flinging his arms around weaving tales for Vernon. They both had big plastic cups. I caught a few glimpses of Vernon dropping his chin and waggling his head in disbelief over whatever was being said and then taking another swallow.

Alva's new swamp boat seemed pristine compared to ours as we pulled alongside. His sported headlights. Wow! Anyway, after storytelling about Pop's wound, things settled down. The men lit on the porch and allowed me some free time.

It had been a very long, hot day. We were all sweaty. The beer had flowed from my hand to the Duck-kateers through most of it, and now they were hitting the brown liquor. I marveled at their capacity. They never seemed to get too tipsy, impaired to the point they couldn't be trusted to drive the boat or handle a gun, only louder and funnier in their banter. That suited me fine. That meant they would forget about me and my status as a gofer. While they sat on the porch watching the sunset, I went to the shade at the back door to crack a new science fiction novel. It was by one of my favorite authors, Anne McCaffrey, called Dragonquest. I was thoroughly engrossed when the Command Bellow drowned out the other voices.

"Boy, take Alva and go check the catfish lines. He's driving us nuts. We need some fish for supper. Alva, git in my boat."

"Whatever you sh-shay, Dick." He trundled over and took a wobbly step down into *his* boat."

"Alva, I said to git in *my* boat. Crawl on over there. Bait's in my cooler." Alva swung his legs over into our boat and sat heavily on the front seat with a grunt.

"Don't forget to re-bait the hooks, and don't cut your fingers off either. One lame person is enough for this weekend."

"Sh-shure thing, Dick. L-let's go, Ricky, before he comes up with something else for usssh to do."

I climbed into the back and started 'er up, thinking that Alva would be hard put not to slice his fingers while cutting up the bait. I resolved to give him a hand. After watching Pop get mauled this afternoon, my own fear of slicing myself filled me with caution.

Granddaddy Boyette sprang to mind as I drove up into Long Pond. I recalled helping him shuck corn from his garden back when I was about ten years old. He was a butcher by profession and knew how to hone knives to a razor's edge. Granddaddy had been showing me how to cut the tops and bottoms off the corn ears with one of his wickedly sharp homemade knives when he laid his middle finger open to the bone. Blood had spilled all over the basket of corn between his knees, his arm, and all over his shirt. Some had even spurted on my cheek. Horrified, I had watched him calmly reach for a strip of cotton cloth to bind his finger. I noticed that he had many strips hanging from a clip on his shop bench, probably just for this purpose. I had asked him if the cut hurt. He had replied, "This is nothing. I've sliced my fingers so many times, I don't even feel it anymore. See?" And he showed all the scars on his gnarled old fingers. It had given me the willies to realize that his fingers weren't twisted with age but from years of self-injury.

Lines were popping up and down as we came into Long Pond. The first thing Alva jerked out of the water was a three-foot-long greenish eel. It was released, too snake-like. Next, we both had to pull up a large, nasty snapping turtle that had probably dug itself under a root. It had swallowed the bait deep into its gullet – too dangerous to try and extract the hook. I recently learned that a common snapping turtle's beak had a bite pressure of one thousand pounds per square inch in biology class. Those big devils could shear off a few fingers. We were forced to cut the line and let it go. Next, we drew out a mudfish. It weighed at least twenty pounds and had nickel-sized scales. Mudfish, *Amia calva*, also known as bowfin, mud pike, dogfish, swamp bass, or cypress trout, dates back a hundred and eighty million years, making it the most ancient species alive today in Lake Marion. They look somewhat like catfish, but the meat is not very tasty, and they have those thick scales instead of skin.

Finally, we started retrieving catfish, two rinky-dink little slimeballs at maybe a pound each. They were the perfect size for pan-frying, but with three big men and a growing boy, we were going to be hard put to make a stew.

Alva said, "Looks like we'll have to use this big old fossil fish to get a stew tonight, Ricky." He and I must have been thinking along the same lines. The mudfish did not look very appetizing.

We got all the hooks checked, applied fresh bait where needed, and returned to the houseboat with our haul. Amazingly, Pop and Vernon were busy in the kitchen. It was almost sundown, so I used the waning light to skin the catfish, scale the mudfish, and produce fillets for the stew. Alva turned on the porch light and brought his flashlight to give me enough light to finish. The cleaning table was mounted between iron roof supports, which allowed it to hang over the water. It had a kitchen sink on the left side with a plastic drum pump to draw swamp water for rinsing and cleanup. Alva and I were just finishing when we received our next command.

"Hurry up with the fish, boys. Me and Vee Bee are getting hungry."

In went the meat. Stew was made and eaten. The big boys and I attempted to view the stars before bed, but my added weight to the front with all of them sitting there caused the left pontoon to sink below the surface. Water washed through the open door. It felt like the houseboat was going to flip over. The men jumped to the right as I hastily retreated to the kitchen area. The water subsided and the houseboat stabilized.

"Looks like we're gonna have to put an extra barrel or two under this thing next trip," said Pop. "Till then, I suggest we don't huddle up on the left side of the front porch."

Vernon asked, "What d'ya thinks causin' it, Dick?"

"Well Vee Bee, you recall those sorry bastards that broke in last year? They blew the locks off the door with a shotgun. I suspect they tried to sink the houseboat after they got done stealing us blind. You can see a couple of BB holes in the left pontoon if you look hard enough. I'll bet there are a few holes below the waterline too."

Alva said, "But Dick – since we filled the pontoons with floatation foam, would it really matter if there were holes?"

"I would say that water could probably leak through the hole or holes and fill air pockets in the foam, sort of like a sponge. It must have added enough extra weight to let this side sink. We don't want to see this baby go down like the last one."

On that note, we all went to bed. Because it was so hot and humid, both doors and windows were thrown open in hopes of catching a cool night breeze. In the middle starboard bunk, I lay atop my blue K-mart sleeping bag in nothing but my underwear, stewing in my own sweat. Moonlight streamed through the front door bouncing off the pale, shirtless torsos of Pop and Alva across the aisle. Alva sprawled in the bottom bunk, Pop in the middle bunk. Looking over the edge of my bunk, I saw Vernon struggle for a comfortable position in the tight space of his bunk.

Alva started making his usual whimpers, "Weeebbbeeebeebeee...weebbbeeebeebee..."

Pop snorted rhythmically with a follow-up, "Shoooboooboooboooo."

Vernon began to snore in a classic burr.

About the time my eyes finally prepared to close despite the noise, a new high-pitched buzz near my ear snapped me fully awake. I listened intently as the minute sound drew closer...and closer.

"Zzzzzzzzz...it!"

Smack.

I killed a mosquito on my right cheek.

"Zzzzzzzzz...it!"

I killed another on my forehead.

The sound of those little vampires increased by the second. I smacked and smacked, to no avail. The onslaught continued. I grabbed my flashlight from where I had placed it on the bunk above. Switching it on, what to my eyes should appear but tiny horrors greater than any yet, I fear. There were hordes of mosquitos drifting through the front door, following the trail of carbon dioxide from my own exhalations. I swung my flashlight around to see if the others were being attacked while they slept. Yes, it seemed that they were.

Mosquitos by the hundreds hovered over the bare bellies of the men, not alighting to draw blood. Instead, those same bugs would eventually give up and start drifting toward me – toward the only designated driver in the bunch. My flesh must have been sweet in comparison to the soused ones snoring obliviously. What was I to do?

My skin was already greasy with insect repellent, but the mosquitoes were not deterred. It was as if I wore perfume. I clamored into my sleeping bag, zipped it, and stuffed the lips under my head to seal it off. I was effectively mummified inside a cloth sack designed to keep me warm in 25-degree weather. It felt like the steam room at the YMCA.

Hoo-whoo, went the choo-choo as it thundered across the trestle, groan-grunt went the alligator, splish-splash went the catfish lines, plop-kerplop went the cypress nuts, and the snores, oh the snores....

"Rise and shine, boys. It's a bright and beautiful day here at Santee. Holy Gamolee!"

I poked my head out of my bag. Pop was standing in the aisle wearing only his skives with his mouth hanging open.

"Just look at all the skeeters! We're gonna have to fumigate before breakfast. Y'all hurry up and get dressed."

While the men plugged up the aisle clothing themselves, I was left to swelter until they finished. Blearily, I observed the thousands of needle-nosed terrors clinging to the walls. It had been the longest night of my life, a night of Homeric torture by the littlest of creatures. I had resisted, endured, tolerated, sweated, itched, slapped, ignored, bunkered, and persevered against the nocturnal opus the likes of which I never, ever wish to repeat. No wonder someone can go mad from torture. Gleefully I ushered the men out to the boats, seized the can of insecticide from the cabinet below the sink, and triumphantly struck a blow to the insect world! Life was full of little unexpected pleasures.

"Home is Heaven for beginners."
~ Charles H. Parkhurst

What Now?

As time wore on and I grew into my late teens, I recognized that hunting in and of itself meant nothing. Having a good bird shoot took preparation, study, practice, and lots of luck. Birds never dove into the pot of their own accord. I was fortunate that Pop and his buddies were all good hunters willing to teach me the necessary skills. Still, I understood that becoming a hunter represented adopting a whole philosophy of living. I was encouraged to be involved with all sorts of team sports, karate, Boy Scouts, lifesaving courses, science classes, U.S. History, conservation, and much more. What all these subjects had in common were shared ethics with those of hunting.

When it came time to duck hunt at the new spot below the trestle in the latter part of 1975, Pop's hand was back in shooting form except for a puckered scar. The weather at Santee was cold, rainy, overcast, foggy – perfect duck weather. This kind of climate slows the birds down from sixty to a mere forty miles per hour, brings them skimming low over the swamp, offering a slightly easier target than usual. In better weather, ducks fly high and fast. Skill and much practice are required to drop a duck with a scattering of tiny pellets spouted from a metal tube.

It was four in the morning. We were decked out, underway, heading for the trestle at idle speed in the pitch dark. Vernon and Brad followed us in their boat. Their V-hull was whirring along on a fifteen-horse motor Vernon had dubbed *Mighty Mite*. I held our new twelve-volt halogen spotlight, the Big Beam, wired to the boat battery. The fog was so thick…wait for it…that it acted as a mirror, reflecting our mighty radiance back in our faces.

"Turn off the big light! I can't see!" yelled Pop. I switched it off and swapped it for the old D-cell standby. Well, at least my eyeballs were thankful for the relief.

Apparently, Pop was going to have to *will* our way to the trestle. Lately, he had been nagging me about using my willpower to achieve my goals. I attempted to *will* a hole in the fog, although I had not yet been trained by Jedi Master Yoda from George Lucas'

Star Wars in the ways of the Force. That wouldn't happen until '77 – what a shame.

"I can't see the Burnetts' boat," I said.

"Don't worry about them. They'll be along. Keep your eyes peeled for the trestle. I don't want to hit it."

The water was low that weekend. There would be a hefty flow trying to pass through beneath the picket of railroad pylons. Speaking of which, one of the massive, creosoted supports materialized out of the fog. By some miracle, our boat slipped right under the trestle without hitting any of the numerous crossbeams. Pop was so relieved, he cut the motor to take a breather.

I could now hear the buzzing of *Mighty Mite* somewhere behind us. It seemed that the Burnett's boat was moving back and forth.

"Sounds like they're trying to find a clear way through the trestle, Pop."

"Yeah, it does." Our voices were muffled. I suppose heavy fog dampens a lot of things. I know I was dripping.

Minutes passed.

KABLAM!

It was the sound of something heavy crashing against something immovable.

From far off, Brad's voice arose, "Daddy, watch out! Back up. Back up!"

Mighty Mite buzzed some more, then WHAM!

"You hit it again, Daddy!"

"Tell me something I don't know, harrumph."

More buzzing from the little motor, then BAM, KABLAM!

"Dammit!"

"Watch out, Daddy. Watch out!"

WHAM! Splutter, splut, splut.

What followed was a string of cussing and fuming and harrumphing. Pop and I sat in silence, waiting patiently for our comrades to catch up. We could now hear paddle strokes.

"We're clear, Daddy."

Once more, *Mighty Mite* was buzzed. Finally, it seemed their boat was getting closer. Pop turned our searchlight behind us to give them a target. This spritely torch could bring the light of day to the deepest gloom in the swamp up to a mile away during any usual darkness. Now, it barely penetrated the fog ten feet behind us. It must have been enough, for a couple of minutes later, the bow of the Burnett's craft sidled up out of the mist. It looked like the crumpled snout of a bulldog.

Brad's face became visible next. He wore a disgruntled look. "It wasn't my fault. Daddy's driving." It's the only time I ever heard Brad say anything remotely negative about his father. Unintelligible grumbling erupted from the back of their boat.

Pop chanced a snicker. "Well, Vee Bee, at least you ain't sunk. Let's go find some ducks!"

Navigating in the fog was a bit easier from that point since we were cutting across the current. We reached the tree line after another ten minutes or so. From there, we snugged up near the trestle, slipping our boats into the hidden little pond Pop and I had discovered back in the spring. Vernon and Brad deployed a couple of hundred feet further up from us. We put out decoys, covered ourselves with camouflage, and waited patiently.

The fog clung.

Time stretched.

Eventually, the darkness became lightness.

Pop and I could hear wings whistling all around but couldn't make out even a shadow of a bird. It was frustrating to know that ducks were out there somewhere.

Pop got antsy. "VEEEEEE BEEEEEE?"

"Yeaaaaaahhh?"

"CAN'T SEE TO SHOOT. LET'S GO GET SOME BREAKFAST AT THE HOUSEBOAT."

"Yeaaaaaahhh!" We could hear Vernon and Brad starting to pack it in.

Pop and I had just finished retrieving our decoys when the sound of paddles nearby, coming from the direction of the big water, filtered through to us.

"Who's that? Vernon and Brad are in the other direction."

"Don't know," Pop said, "Might be another boatload of hunters."

"Nope," came a short reply, but not from me.

Another jon boat approached from out of the fog. Two men wearing official-looking garb peered at us. The passenger reached over to grab our gunnel.

The driver said, "Game wardens. Pull out your licenses and your boat registration."

"Awwww, come on. We haven't even fired a shot this morning," said Pop. "We were just leaving."

"Licenses and registration, then show us your guns," was the curt reply. I noticed that both wardens carried pistols on their hips and badges pinned to the chest pockets of their coats. Each wore broad-brimmed official-looking hats too. They were not smiling. "Sir, why were your running lights off before sunrise?"

Pop raised his voice a bit, probably hoping Vernon and Brad would hear. "What sunrise? We can't even see the sun. Anyway, we're hunting ducks. You can't have your running lights on. The ducks will flare."

"Sir," said Passenger Warden, "You were navigating your vessel in the dark with no running lights. This is a violation of South Carolina Boating Regulations and a hazard to other boaters. You will receive a $100 fine."

Pop, still loudly, said, "The fog was so thick; we couldn't see the boat lights anyway. Hell, we could barely even see our 1200-lumen spotlight. We had *that* on. Can't you let us off with a warning?"

Passenger Warden said, "Perhaps we could have if you had shown a little more respect. Don't look so disgusted, son. If you will both cooperate, we'll get finished doing our job a bit sooner, and you can be on your way. Now, *please* pass your weapons over for inspection." He released his hold on our boat and took our guns. While he shucked out the shells, checked the magazine plugs (which prevents loading more than three shells into the shotgun), measured the barrels to ensure they were above minimum regulation length, his partner took our licenses and the boat registration.

Driver Warden looked over the papers. "Show me your driver's license, Mr. Meehan." Pop's face was red, but he pulled it out of his wallet and passed it over without a word. "Do you own this boat, Mr. Meehan?"

"My name's right there on the license and registration," Pop said. Oh yes, he was getting a bit agitated.

"Yes, sir. I see that." Driver Warden looked hard into Pop's face. "I say again, do you own this boat, sir?"

"I do."

"Are you aware, sir, that your registration expires in two days?" Driver Warden cocked an eyebrow. Meanwhile, my gun was returned to me, unloaded. Passenger Warden placed my three legal duck loads into my hand.

"I am. We'll be going home tomorrow."

Passenger Warden spoke to his partner. "Hey, John, take a look at this." He showed John how a fourth shell was nearly able to be pressed into the magazine on my father's Browning automatic. He attempted to force the shell in but failed.

"You're a lucky man, Mr. Meehan," said Warden John. "Another eighth of an inch, and that shell would go in. The fine for more than three shells in the chamber would have been $150, and your gun would have been confiscated. I suggest you get a longer plug." He passed back Pop's gun and shells. "Here's your citation for today. You may pay at the Sumter County Courthouse, or you may mail the payment once you get home. The address of the courthouse is listed on the citation for your convenience. Failure to make payment by the deadline doubles the fine and could include jail time at the judge's discretion. Thank you for your cooperation. Have a nice day."

The two wardens cast themselves off, started their motor, and disappeared into the fog. We could not hear Vernon or Brad, so they must have been lying low.

"Damn wardens," said Pop. "Rick – put the damn bow light on. We're going back to the damn houseboat. Vernon and Brad'll be along eventually." I complied. Pop started our motor, and off we went. We still could barely navigate because of the fog. As we pulled out of the swamp into the big water, the same two wardens swung over toward us again. When they realized we had already been checked, they turned back toward our duck hidey-hole, probably looking for Vernon's boat.

"Damn wardens," Pop repeated. "How much you wanna bet they only stopped us because there's no one else out here hunting this morning?" I exercised restraint and kept my mouth shut. I would have begun figuring up the cost per bird for this trip, but we didn't have any ducks yet.

We got back to the houseboat first. Pop started frying up bacon and boiling some grits while we waited for Vernon and Brad to arrive. Eventually, the crumpled bow materialized out of the fog. The two of them unloaded their gear while Pop and I silently finished making a pile of scrambled eggs.

Finally, Vernon broke the silence. "Humf, well Dick, it weren't a fruitful shoot this mornin'."

"Naw, Vee Bee."

"Did you get fined?"

"Sure did. A hundred smacks."

"Me and Brad stayed put when we heard y'all talking. Them game wardens didn't find us."

"They must be awfully dedicated, Vee Bee, getting out ahead of us this morning. They really had to work in all that fog. Tell you what. Let's just hunt behind the houseboat tonight. I don't feel like taking another long ride."

"Sure, Dick."

The Burned-Out Stump slough turned out to be the perfect spot for the evening shoot. Each of us got a wood duck for dinner. After calculating the expenditures on food, shotgun shells, gasoline for car and boat, licenses, duck stamps, and the fine, I determined that each bird cost about fifty-five bucks. It was nearly dark as we were packing up the decoys when to our ears, the sound of paddles came again.

Pop and I looked at each other. We both started putting decoys in the boat at high speed.

"Good evening, gentlemen." A large light plastered us so we couldn't see. "We meet again."

It was the same game wardens from this morning.

Warden John continued, "Please provide your hunting licenses and boat registration. That goes for you in the other boat, too – paddle on over here. We'll check your information in a minute. Be aware that by our *official* timepiece, you were all shooting after sunset. Your birds are hereby confiscated. Hand your guns over to my partner for inspection."

"Please don't take the ducks. We were going to eat them for supper," said Pop.

"Sir, you should have considered that before you fired your gun after *official* sunset," said Warden John. "Please hand over the carcasses."

"What do y'all do with the meat?" asked Brad.

"We take confiscated birds to a local children's home," said passenger warden.

Each of us received a citation for a hundred dollars. The per bird cost had risen. Now we also had four points off our licenses for shooting after *official* sunset. By my calculations, the per bird cost was now about $170. It was an expensive trip.

What capped the weekend was when the same two wardens stopped us yet again as we were leaving the swamp on Sunday, just before noon. This time they found nothing wrong with either of our boats. All four of us were subdued, respectful, and glad to be going home.

"Maturity is the time of life when, if you had the time, you'd have the time of your life."
~ *Anonymous*

18

Dudes

"Pop, would it be okay if I borrowed your boat to take David down to Santee so we can hunt ducks next weekend?" I didn't sound as confident as I figured to be.

There was a pause before Pop turned his full withering attention to me.

"Did Dick Atherton say it was okay with him for David to go?"

"I haven't heard back from David yet."

"Well, it's okay with me, Son. I expect Dick will have something to say about it, though. It's a big step."

A thrill shot through me. Having turned sixteen a few months back, getting my permanent driver's license with no restrictions – it was the year for giant steps. I wondered if David got permission from his dad. The question had not grown cold when the black rotary dial wall phone rang.

"My dad hasn't given permission yet," David said anxiously. "He wants to talk to your dad first."

"I'm sure it'll be okay. Pop told me this morning we could go." I really wasn't as confident as I tried to sound. Mr. G. Richard "Dick" Atherton, with the same nickname as my father, intimidated me almost as much as Pop did. He was totally different from other dads I knew. He seemed more somber. It was years before I began to understand his droll humor.

That same evening, the phone rang again. Pop picked up on the extension beside his favorite chair in the den.

"Hiya, Dick. Yeah, Ricky asked me this morning. I told him it was okay with me. Sure. Sure. I wouldn't have given my permission if I didn't think they could handle it. You know me, Dick, trained up right. Nothing to worry about. Glad we had David with us on all those hunting trips. Never been any trouble at all. He's a great young man. See you at Lion's Club tomorrow. Bye now." I heard the receiver hang up. "RICK!"

I scrambled into the den from the kitchen. "Yes, sir?"

"That was Dick Atherton."

"Yes, sir."

"He wasn't too gung-ho about you and David going to Santee without me."

My heart sank.

"I convinced him it would be okay, but it was touch and go there for a minute. You boys be really careful and don't make me out to be a liar – get me?"

"Yes, sir!" Excitement rose in my chest until I couldn't stand still. "We'll take good care of your stuff, and we'll be careful. Thank you, Pop!"

"Alright." His eyes drilled into me. "Don't disappoint me, Son. It's my reputation on the line."

"We won't, Pop."

"Be careful. Be safe. Don't destroy my boat!"

"We will, Pop." That didn't sound quite right. "I mean, we won't."

"I know what you mean. Give me your word."

I mustered up some courage, walked over to have my hand engulfed. Giving what I believed was a firm handshake, I promised to be careful and not damage anything, especially neither David nor myself.

Lately, Pop had been teaching me about integrity and its importance to one's reputation. The old saw, "My word is my bond," came up often. "Protect your reputation jealously, Son. It's all you've got; it's the only thing you truly own."

A few months my junior, David William Atherton, in school with me from Day One, came over to the house to help figure out the gear we would take to Santee. We prepared the boat, planned the meals and drinks, and generally confabbed to make sure we didn't forget anything important. Spare batteries, the searchlight, enough No. 4 duck loads, and a hundred other little things were checked, double checked, and triple checked. We knew we were ready. The excitement was palpable all the way down to Pack's Landing.

It was freedom from adult supervision.

It was a time of firsts.

First, we nearly sunk the boat as we were putting in at Pack's because we forgot to remove the nylon safety strap holding the craft firmly on the trailer. Water flooded over the transom for a bit, but the boat decided to float even with the trailer still strapped to it. We scratched our heads for a few moments until it became apparent what we had done wrong.

First, we pulled the boat out, drained the water through the inch-diameter port at the bottom of the transom, and removed the offending nylon tiedown strap. We then tried to relaunch the boat, only this time it filled up with water because we had forgotten to reinstall the drain plug in the bottom of the transom. Most jon boats have removable drain plugs so bilgewater can be ejected.

First, we sheared a pin on a stump right out in the middle of Pack's Flats as we crossed over toward the Leaning Tree. We had to hang over the prop to replace the pin while bobbing up and down.

First, we got lost up at the end of Long Pond trying to get to the houseboat because some of our license plate markers were just below the waterline this trip. When we finally did arrive at the houseboat, we thought we had forgotten the key to one of the two different padlocks on the front door. Then the twelve-volt lights did not light, but luckily, as the son of a professional electrician, David knew to sand the corrosion off the battery terminals and clips. He used a piece of steel wool Pop always kept in the toolbox for cleaning the motor spark plugs.

That first night we got our hands on a nearly fresh copy of our first Playboy magazine, which had been left on the table by the last visitors, probably my dad and Dr. Pack. Miss July tantalized us from her prominent place pinned to the wall. In this privileged spot, she resided in timeless beauty for many years. We discovered our first bottle of Jack Daniels sitting on the table as well. It was enlightening, to say the least.

We sat out on the porch by ourselves late into the night for the first time, enjoying Swisher Sweet cigarillos and whiskey. We could have shot Pop's obnoxious windup alarm clock that rattled the daylights out of us an hour early, 3:45 a.m. instead of 4:45. We were too excited to go back to sleep. Besides, the train crossed the trestle about then for the first time this trip. Everything around us shimmied from the combination of the incredible decibel level of the horn and the massive weight rumbling across the wooden trestle through our wintery water-land. So, we got busy loading up the boat for our first independent duck hunt, youthful stamina fully engaged in the wee hours.

Behind the houseboat at the Burned-Out Stump slough was our chosen location for the morning hunt. We clamored into our heaviest duck weather gear, donned our vinyl hooded ponchos because the rain had begun to fall heavily, carried, and deployed thirty decoys, stretched miles of camo cloth over everything, siphoned a thermos of hot Campbell's Cream of Mushroom Soup, held our new Remington 1100 shotguns, gifts from our fathers, and sat patiently still.

Pop's old clock was a tick-tocking menace after it stopped keeping time. That didn't deter him from using it anyway.

Two hours early.

Pitch black, no stars, no moon – the heavy rain became a steady drizzle.

Cold.

Wet and getting wetter.

Ducks began to fly at 6:52 A.M., but the official sunrise wasn't until 7:29. We let them pass by unmolested, as required by law. Grouping after grouping whizzed over as we sipped our soup and huddled under our ponchos. We checked our watches.

7:27

7:28

7:29 – Eureka!

Let's shoot. Okay. David faced south. I faced north. Using peripheral vision so we wouldn't move too much, we covered three hundred sixty degrees as a team. No bird would pass through without a warning whisper.

7:30

8:00

9:00

Not a single bird flew close enough to shoot. We packed it in. No big deal. We'd head back and get some breakfast, then put out the catfish lines. There would be no Saturday night supper unless we shot it or caught it, following the tradition set forth by our elders. Otherwise, our pickings would be slim, potato chips coupled with less savory fare. Maybe we'd have better luck for the afternoon hunt, but a nap right after lunch was in order.

It stopped raining, but the skies remained broody. The catfish were not biting. We re-baited the lines just past noon in hopes that the "fresh" rotten mullet would attract them better.

Then, we headed to the Brambles for the evening shoot. This was a forty-five-minute trip up the flats, or through Long Pond, the scenic route. Since we had several hours before we needed to be set for ducks, we took the scenic route.

The rainfall had caused the water to rise. Only a few stumps were visible. The rest lurked at or just below the surface. We hit many, some hard enough to add yet another dent to the bottom of Pop's boat. I cringed each time. Still, even under gray skies, the beauty of the swamp made such things as the next broken cotter key a mere nuisance, not a deterrent. Fixing that, we continued following the marked trail, paralleling Pack's Flats toward Rimini.

Eventually, we meandered across the westerly trail leading to the Brambles, so named because of the acres of heavy sticklike brush poking out of the water. As I guided us up the marked trail, David lurched to starboard, my signal to turn the opposite way immediately. A quick push of my arm was all it took.

The boat arced to the right.

The boat lurched atop some hidden obstruction on one side, then the other.

The boat stabilized as if sitting on dry land.

The motor choked off.

The two of us could not shift the boat at all, no matter how we distributed or combined our weight. We were stuck. After a few minutes, the water settled a bit. We could make out what appeared to be a double row of stumps, perfectly round at about sixteen inches in diameter, cut flat on top. They traversed the swamp from northwest to southeast in a straight line. And we were settled on four of them, two in the front and two in the back. We weren't going anywhere.

"Goob, what do you think this is?" David asked. Ever since he discovered that *goober pea* was another name for peanut, that became my nickname. It was a whole lot better than other names people were calling me at the school, such as Meathead and Me-butt. I could live with Goob. Absolutely.

I rummaged through the toolbox for our lake map. "I think it may be an old railroad spur. Pop says they run all through the swamp. He calls them *tramlines*. Let me find the map and we'll take a look. He's marked some of the lines. He also told me that they logged all the big cypress trees using flatcars pulled by steam engines before building the dam. I'm gonna check the map to see if this spur is on it. If not, I'll draw it in."

David said, "That makes sense. We don't want to keep hitting it when we come to the Brambles. Wouldn't it have been something if we ran over it in the dark?"

I found the tramline marked on the map as an almost invisible route with hundreds of little crosses representing a railroad track. It wasn't my first trip to the Brambles, but it was the first time hitting this underwater menace. Of course, each day at Santee *is* unique. I suppose the water level happened to be just right to cause our current predicament.

We were stuck fast out in the middle of a rare area devoid of trees, stumps, or pigweed. Paddles were useless because we couldn't reach the bottom to gain purchase in the mud. The pylons were beneath us, so we couldn't even push against them. It was a conundrum. Since we weren't in a big hurry yet to get to the Brambles, we kept looking for alternatives besides the obvious – climbing into the water and attempting to shove the boat free.

David said, "I see a little snag sticking up about twenty feet in front of us. Maybe we can lasso it with the bow rope and pull ourselves off."

I crawled forward to see what he was talking about. "That's a small stob," I said, "but let's give it a try. I really don't want to go for a swim."

David tied a slip knot at the end of our bow rope and spent the next half hour trying to toss the loop over the stob. "I give, pal. It's your turn."

I took the rope, stood on the bow seat, and let fly. Once. Twice. The third time was the charm. The loop dropped neatly over the little stob.

"You lucky sucker," said David.

"No luck to it. That was skill," I rejoined. "Let's see if it can be pulled tight without coming off again." The slipknot did its job of tightening when we started tugging. Unbelievably, we were both able to pull against the thin little stob, and although it flexed, it did not snap. Soon we were straining for all we were worth. Inch by inch, the boat slipped over the pylons until, with a final lurch, we floated free. It was around 4:00 p.m. We had been trying to rescue ourselves for almost three hours.

"We da men!" David gave me a low five.

"We're gonna be hungry men if we don't get any birds or catfish this evenin'." I was glad we didn't have to swim. Another twenty minutes of riding and we made it to the Brambles. Another twenty after that, we had deployed our decoys and covered ourselves behind our favorite fallen tree.

Darkness crept in early thanks to the heavy cloud cover. Flurries of ducks began to cross the tree lines. I pulled out my latest duck call, a whistle made from a spent twelve-gauge shell. Pop had shown me how to cut it off at an angle with my pocketknife. By holding the shell against my lips and blowing across its edge, I could produce a compelling wood duck whistle that uplifted in pitch just like the real birds. Lured by my call, a large group came sailing low and steady over our decoys. We each took a woodie before the group climbed frantically away. For the first time, I had called birds down to the decoys. It was indeed a confidence booster; hence, we began to use our new favorite mantra.

"We came. We saw. We conquered." David high-fived me this time.

"Cool, man," I chimed in.

As legal hunting hours ended, we stopped shooting to allow several *rafts* to land in our decoys. As Pop had pointed out once, at that point they became a *paddling*, because they paddle around as a group while searching for food. Ducks are fascinating creatures as they glide in for a landing – at once wholly vulnerable and graceful.

I spun us around to head back, mainly concerned that we didn't get caught up on that tramline again. We would have to make sure not to cross it accidentally in the dark. David held the flashlight at the ready. He was probably thinking the same thing.

The Brambles shrank away in the growing darkness behind us. As the temperature dropped, a layer of fog quickly developed around us. Our flashlight became useless. It could barely penetrate more than two feet of the white veil in front of the bow. We bumped and jolted spasmodically as it became impossible to avoid unseen obstacles.

"Pea soup!" David yelled.

The author in cold-weather gear

"Shine the light around and see if you can spot the marker. We should be right on top of it!"

I happened to have guessed right. One thing about rectangles of chopped-up old license plates, they make great reflectors even in foggy weather. I breathed a sigh as one after another reflected the flashlight every thirty yards or so. Gradually the forests fell to the sides as the cut emptied into the open water of the flats. We were glad to have missed the tramline, but now waves of fog, buffeted by a slight breeze, made the whole world seem eerie. We headed down toward the railroad trestle, hugging the trees that separated the flats from the real swamp. Pop had once told me there were fewer stumps to hit along here. That was flawed information. We kept hitting the prop on underwater stumps every half minute. It became unnerving as the gloom deepened.

"Hey, David! I can't see the bow light. Did you put it on? We have to have lights on after dark. I'm sure the game wardens would love to ticket us." We had both forgotten. I became a bit self-conscious to realize I was yelling over the drone of the motor. I had learned that water conducted sound quite well, and most of what we said was probably heard clearly by anyone within several miles of us. We were not only telling everyone that we were lost, but that we were not legal. I quickly dropped us to idle speed and threw the motor into neutral. While David disentangled the light from somewhere under his feet and started mounting it, I clamped the stern light to the transom.

For non-boaters, the bow light was like a flashlight in that it ran on a D-cell battery, but it had one green lens on the right (starboard) and one red lens on the left (port). Coupled with the stern white light, which was also run by a battery, other boaters could judge the orientation of oncoming craft even in the darkness. Not necessarily in pea soup, however. I could barely see David's shadowy form.

"Find the Leaning Tree," I called. This was a tall, dead cypress trunk wedged between two shorter brothers. The way it leaned resembled a giant finger pointing to our cut. I began to angle the boat closer to the tree line to look for it.

David raised the flashlight higher to the right. I was relieved to see the Leaning Tree above the layer of fog. I turned into our cut.

"Now find me the Three Giants."

The breeze had increased enough to push the fog out into the flats, now behind us. The Three Giants, our next trail marker, had to be kept on our port side to avoid stumps. Sliding past these behemoth side-by-side trees always told me that we were nearly back to the houseboat. I felt safer as we entered the first run through a cypress stand. Before the dam was built, this was probably a stream that meandered through the swamplands to the main river. By following markers, we made our way without mishap around what would have been glades, and then another stand of trees, winding among the wide trunks in the darkness, until we came out at our run to the houseboat. The run amounted to a long pond between tree lines. Pop named it thus years ago. During daylight, Long Pond displayed great natural beauty. In the darkness, it represented an obstacle to cross.

After another short run through the woods, twisting this way and that, we arrived at our haven. The houseboat was nestled between four large cypress trees, permanently moored with inch-thick steel cables. There was a cleat mounted to the porch for tying off the boat. As I did so, all uneasiness left me. We were back at last to safety and comfort.

Duck Tale

After getting stuck on the tram line yesterday, David and I decided to give Sparkleberry Cut a whirl today. The weather had cleared overnight, so the swamp showed its full glory in the early sunshine. Our unsuccessful morning hunt over, we checked the catfish lines, then swung by the houseboat to grab breakfast. Next, we headed out to explore regions that weren't particularly familiar to us. I had in mind a destination I had seen only twice before, an area of unforgettable natural beauty.

"We've found them. Right through there is the Hall of Giants," I asserted. The heavy current and breadth of the passage into the cypress forest told me that this had once been a tributary off the main river. We were traveling upstream in clear water, winding around through an ancient, heavily wooded, cypress forest. These trees must have been spared by the loggers back in the early thirties.

We cruised through the majestic gallery until we came upon a bit of dry land to starboard. This was a decent spot to enjoy lunch, stretch our legs, and relieve ourselves before turning back. Then, we discovered something odd.

Someone else had parked a jon boat not more than forty feet further upstream. Since we had neither seen nor heard another boat or person all day, we decided to walk over and check it out. The boat was full of water. Its bow rope was not tied off to anything, so the boat was only held in place by its position on the muddy bank. The gas tank was floating. I lifted it – empty. There was a cooler. When David opened it, the smell of death rolled over us. The food inside was decomposed as if it had been rotting for weeks. He hastily closed the lid. A paddle and a boat cushion were in place as if the owner intended to return shortly.

Author in Hall of Giants

"I think we should go," David said. He looked pale and anxious, probably the same way I looked.

That was my inclination too, but I mustered some courage. "What if someone is up in here hurt and needing help? Maybe we should search around to see. We do have our guns with us."

"What if he has a gun too?"

"Let's just get our guns and search around. We can always run for it." I smiled while trying to seem confident. One thing was sure, that boat was too nice to have been abandoned out in the middle of nowhere. Something was definitely wrong.

We grabbed our shotguns and stuffed extra ammo in our pockets, then pushed through the underbrush beneath the trees out to about two hundred feet in front of our boat. Arcing around to the left, we finally stopped. It was useless to keep pushing through. We simply couldn't see a thing.

"Let's yell and see if he answers," I said.

David nodded.

I said, "On the count of three, we yell 'Hey.' One…two…three…HEEEEEYYYYY."

Our voices rolled down through the empty forest. There was no reply. We tried several more times without a response, so we went back to our boat.

"I think what we'll do is go report this at Pack's Landing. The game wardens may want to come check it out," I said.

"Agreed. Let's get the hell out of here. This place is giving me the creeps."

It did feel as if the Hall of Giants was closing in upon us as we left the vicinity of the abandoned boat. Once we exited the corridor back into the more open trails through Sparkleberry, the sun warmed our faces and dispelled our fears. Only, we began to have a little difficulty finding our way back toward Rimini. The angles of the shadows among the trees tended to hide the trail markers, and the pigweed had shifted dramatically since we had passed earlier, effectively concealing our trail. The only thing that remained the same was the heavy flow of water. I purposefully went with the flow, knowing it would eventually lead us back to Pack's Flats.

"We've been going around in circles," said David after a while.

"No, we haven't," I said. "We've been heading in the direction of the flats. See the water flow?" I knew we were headed in the right direction, although it would have made me more comfortable to find some trail markers. I decided to play it cool. "See the angle of the sun? Notice the flow of the water? We're heading back the way we came."

"Bull. It's almost three. It gets dark around six. I don't want to end up running out of gas and spending the night in the swamp like your dad and Dr. Pack did the last time they came down."

"That won't happen. I know exactly where I am," and I did too, well, mostly. But I was up to baiting David a little. Pop and Dr. Pack had gotten lost up in the Riser's Dead Lake area. That was supposedly miles above the Hall of Giants, but I hadn't been that far yet.

I said, "Look, the sun's setting on our right, that puts Pack's about ten o'clock on our left."

"You don't know where we are. We're just meandering around. When the sun goes down, we won't find our way out." The strain in his voice was becoming too much for me. He seemed to be getting angry. I suppose I needed to show some compassion.

"Okay, little lost boy, I'll show you the way home." I smiled. David scowled. "Do you see the rectangle on that tree over there? All we have to do is find the next one." I was relieved to see that marker myself. Now, if we could just keep finding them despite having to continually circumvent islands of pigweed.

David rubbernecked. "There's one." He pointed. Shortly, he pointed to another. The sun was indeed declining, and I did want to get to Pack's and report that abandoned boat and still have enough time to make the evening hunt in the Brambles. I increased our speed.

Eventually, we wound our way into the top of Long Pond. That wasn't exactly where I believed we were, but I felt secure knowing we had made it into familiar territory. Somehow, we had even missed hitting that tramline too. When we scooted out into the flats, the relief emanating from my friend was palpable.

I was familiar with the feeling, as I had experienced it numerous times growing up. I smiled at his back. This was, after all, only our first trip to Santee on our own. We were just stretching our legs, reaching for adulthood. Experiences of this type elicited what I've heard described as the indomitable Spirit of Man. Each tiny success in the wilderness gave David and me more confidence in our abilities. Perhaps that is the leading character trait enhanced through hunting: Confidence.

When we got back home, Pop came out to help us unload the boat. "Well, did you bust anything?"

David and I replied together, "No, sir."

"Well, did you get any ducks?"

"Yes, sir. I got two," said David, "and Ricky only got one. All of them were wood ducks." He smirked at me.

"We caught a couple of big catfish too," I said.

"I don't see any meat in the cooler here. What did you do with all the birds and fish?"

"We ate them," said David.

"I suppose you didn't starve then. Did everything go okay? Did you have any trouble?"

I looked David square in the eye when I answered for us, "Everything was great." After all, what happens at Santee, stays at Santee.

"Man is the only animal that blushes. Or needs to."
~ Mark Twain

| 19 |

Under the Influence

I stood at the small dinner table inside the houseboat, flipping through the latest *Playboy* magazine when Vernon sidled up to me.

"Errr...Rick...can I...uuuh...can I talk to you for a minute?" He was obviously under some sort of stress as he peered up at me through his silver wire rims.

"Sure, Vernon." I folded the magazine closed as discretely as possible, trying not to allow myself to blush at having been caught perusing smut. I gave him my full attention.

"Er, yer daddy told me you've got a real pretty girlfriend, ah Penny. He says y'all have been datin' hot 'n heavy for a while now." Sweat trickled from beneath his sideburns. "You've got him scared."

"Scared? What do you mean?" I couldn't imagine anything scaring Pop.

"I'm just a-sayin'." He paused to mop his face using a handkerchief produced from his back pocket. "He, ahhh, oooh, he wanted me to talk with you a bit about da birds and da bees. He don't want you gittin' duh girl pregnant, you know? Make sure to use a condom and all that. Better yet, keep everything in your underwear."

Ahem. Now I understood. Surely my head was going to explode any moment. I dropped my eyes to study the faded carpet. "Y-yes, sir. I will. I mean, Penny and I, we're not, um, we're not *doing* it."

"That sho' will make yer daddy feel better." He reached up and gave my shoulder a pat, "Better to wait till yer married anyhow." He clumped back to the porch.

I remained rooted to the floor.

Past dates with Penny began to swirl around my head as I sought instances that would have given Pop the wrong, or in all honesty, the *right* impression.

I expect it was easy for him to figure it out. Lately, Penny Leigh Wyant had become my high school sweetheart. Eventually, I moved on to another, then another, and yet another – finally landing on my soul mate and mother of my children, Renee. But for now, Pretty Penny was the girl for me.

During marching season, I discovered that we were both involved with the Spartanburg High School Band. Her figure caught my eye one day during practice, and I nearly split my lip on my saxophone mouthpiece when my jaw dropped. She was marching down the field with the color guard, wearing a tight, short outfit, twirling her old gold and navy school flag. Penny was well-endowed, or as we used to say, *stacked*. I worked up the nerve to ask her out, and she became my steady date.

What doubtless prompted this strange encounter with a third party, Vernon Burnett, was what I had done with Penny just last weekend. Now, Pop loved his Chevy Suburban. It was one of the earliest models, a two-ton truck with a four-wheel-drive transmission, orange-tan with a broad white stripe across the sides. It *never* got stuck in the mud. He was proud of that vehicle, but he let me borrow it for my date with Penny. I planned to take her out to Croft State Park lake for a picnic, among other things. She wore more of those tight short-shorts and a bikini tank top. It was no wonder what happened next. At least, I've always told myself that.

Here we were, she far across the front seat, me proudly driving the Big Hunting Vehicle, heading downhill on a country road lined with stately white pines. Penny slid over next to me and laid her arms lovingly on my shoulder and across my swelling chest. It surprised me enough to draw my attention down to her own, barely contained, swelling breasts.

WHUMP!

I turned my attention back to the road – which was no longer there.

WHUMP, WHUMP, WHUMP!

The car bucked and jolted.

Penny shrieked just like in a horror flick.

I saw something I could not process. Five or six-inch diameter pine trees were flying up over the hood and roof – branches, roots, and all! I slammed the brake pedal to the floor to no avail. The vehicle was too heavy, and the shoulder of the road was a muddy ditch. We plowed up tree after tree. Eventually, a bunch of them got jammed under the car, grinding us to a halt from sheer weight. Penny was crying, but we were unscathed. The same could not be said about Pop's prized vehicle.

I exited through the driver's door, of course, and pulled Penny out after me. The vehicle was laid over in the ditch at a sharp angle. The motor turned off on its own. While Penny stood beside the door, I walked around the car to survey the damage. There were lots of small pines crammed against the passenger side, a few sticking out from underneath, but the best I could tell, the vehicle wasn't completely destroyed. However, I could plainly see myself in the right-side mirror, lodged in the bark of a pine tree directly in front of my face. I looked haggard.

After pulling as many uprooted saplings from the front of the vehicle as I could, thinking hard about what I was going to say to Pop, I helped Penny climb back in so we could try to get the vehicle home. It did start – reluctantly. That was a bad sign. The gearshift gave me a hard time putting it into Drive. I pressed the gas pedal with the utmost care until the Suburban began to crawl out of the ditch. Penny had a white-knuckled grip on the dash.

I did a U-turn and got the Suburban moving back uphill, although the transmission would not shift out of first gear. We were crawling so slow that I got an eyeful of the damage I caused. Fully two hundred feet of ditch and embankment had been torn up by my mistake. Trees were snapped off or uprooted along the entire stretch. I glanced at Penny and knew she was thinking the same thing as I. We were fortunate!

The Suburban limped back home from there, about four miles. Pop had heard us coming and was already standing on the driveway.

The closer the vehicle got, the grimmer his visage became. Things did not bode well.

I had to let Penny out the driver's door again, as her door had been crumpled. Pop was already pacing up and down, surveying the damage. Penny and I came around to face him. I had to hand it to her for her bravery.

Pop stopped pacing and looked us up and down. "Are you two okay? Anything hurt?"

We both answered immediately, "No, sir."

He turned back to the vehicle. "So, are you going to tell me what happened?"

I took a deep breath. "Pop, I only took my eyes off the road for a moment. Next thing I knew, we rolled off into the ditch."

"Where?"

"Right up there on Whitestone-Glendale Road. We were on the way to Croft State Park."

He let off a big breath. "I'm glad nobody got hurt. Where's my mirror?"

Penny said, "It's…it's stuck in a tree, Mr. Meehan."

"Pop, I couldn't get it loose, or I would have brought it back with us."

"Okay, well, why don't you go on inside and get cleaned up a bit. I'm gonna go get my mirror."

"Pop, I couldn't get the transmission to shift gears. We came all the way home in first."

"I heard the whine. That's how I knew you were coming. Just go on in the house. I'll be back shortly."

The Suburban started up without a racket, thank goodness. He backed out of the drive and was gone. Apparently, the transmission only needed a bit of coaxing. Later, he told me that everything checked out fine except the side of the car. He did retrieve the mirror.

That evening, he drove Penny home and let me explain things to her father. He and Mr. Wyant had calmly accepted the whole story. I couldn't understand it. No punishment seemed to be forthcoming. I felt ashamed for my lapse in judgment. When Pop and I returned home, he made one final statement. "Son, I just finished making my last payment yesterday. It took me four years to do it."

About a month later, Pop came home from work in a car that I didn't recognize. He hopped out of the vehicle, grinning. "Hey, what do you think of the *Brown Bomber?*"

This was his Suburban, only now the right side had been beaten out, so the doors worked. The whole shebang was newly painted a dark brown.

"You did me a big favor, Boy. Now I don't have to worry about getting scratches and dents crawling to and from the duck swamps!" He laughed and walked away. That was that.

"We got these sons-a-bitches sitting on the water about 9:00 last night with a flashlight trespassing out of season."
~ Dr. Alva S. Pack, III

20

Pack Rat

Dr. Alva S. Pack, III, entered the hunting sphere contiguous to Pop, not with a whisper but a shout. A little shorter, a little chubbier, the good eye doctor could spew his wit around faster than the green apple quick step. This meant that instead of an inseparable twosome, I now had to deal with the incomparable Three Duck-keteers. As a teenager, I could not compete with them on the comedic score. Apparently, I was just along as the gofer, for I was sitting on the boat's front seat next to the cooler, generally being ignored, except for one other thing.

"Hey Ricky," said Dr. Pack, "pass me a beer. Want one, Vernon?"

"Bub, braha. Git me one too, Rick. How 'bout you, Dick?"

"Does a bear poop in the woods?"

I passed back three cans of beer. If I had to guess, I figured it would be another fifteen minutes before they asked again. Hence, I tuned out the camaraderie to watch a brown squirrel leaping from mossy limb to mossy limb, chattering at being disturbed by the likes of us. It put me in mind of my grandfather.

Brady "Red" Boyette, Pop's stepdad, had once taken me squirrel hunting in a pine forest next to his old neighborhood in Charlotte, North Carolina. I got three using his old 22-caliber rifle. He showed me how to prep and fry them. I had learned that there's not much meat on a squirrel, although what there was of it did taste a little like chicken. I decided those rascally rodents would be worth the effort only if I was starving. [As I wrote this paragraph, six squirrels were fighting over the ripe blueberries on the bushes outside my window. Maybe squirrel stew wouldn't be so bad after all.]

About then, I noticed a large heron lazily winging northward, way up there, almost invisible.

Dr. Pack said, "I'll bet you can't hit it with one shot, Ricky. Y'all want some of this action?"

"His little gun can't reach that far. I'm in, heh, heh, fer a dollar. Easy money." said Vernon.

"I know he can hit it," said Pop. "Shoot it, Boy. Shoot it!"

Blam went my single-shot 20 gauge. Down came the heron from at least a hundred yards high – like a feathered missile, beak first, splashing down right beside the Three Giants.

Silence.

I couldn't believe my eyes. I wouldn't have taken the challenge if I had known I would actually hit the bird. Hunter's Rule #1 tickled the back of my neck.

Alva said, "Can you believe he shot that poor heron, Meehan?"

Vernon said, "Yeah, a heron. All feathers, no meat."

Pop said, "Boy, you know you got to eat what you kill. Y'all pay up."

The banter continued behind my back as the boat glided next to my downed bird. I pulled the ungainly carcass out of the water by one long leg and dropped it in the bottom of the boat.

"I didn't think he would do it," said Alva.

"I didn't think he could do it," said Vernon.

"He knew better'n to shoot it in the first place," said Pop.

I hunkered down in my seat and awaited the inevitable. When we got back to the houseboat, I cleaned the bird. Never had I seen so many feathers – not on a dove, nor a quail, nor a pheasant, nor a goose, nor a duck. This heron was all feathers, neck, and legs, or so it seemed. By the time I got finished, I had at most an ounce of breast meat and half that on both thighs. It got cooked right along with the morning's wood ducks, and now it held a prominent place on my plate. I choked down the stringy, dry meat. Each chew cemented my resolve not to let the three amigos goad me into this type of predicament again. Eat what you kill, indeed. No more heron for me. No, sir. Nor crow, nor robin, nor nothing but *actual* wild game.

Game birds, when prepared correctly, beat chicken hands down. *Vee Bee's Venerable Santee Wood Ducks Over Wild Rice* (see Appendix for recipe) was delicious. I was taught early on not to be squeamish where game animals and fish were concerned. They are good eating, pure and simple. There's nothing different about hunting versus buying meat from an abattoir. Ever been to one? Ever seen cows and chickens being processed for public consumption? The carnage inside an abattoir goes far beyond anything a hunter must deal with. I've got a strong stomach. Still, even I must *will* myself to remain objective in such a place.

"Hey, Ricky," said Dr. Pack, "don't feel too bad about shooting that heron. Your dad can't even see that far. Did I ever tell you how we met?"

"No, sir."

"Your daddy thought he was a big wheel in the Spartanburg Jaycees when I joined in July '69. He talked to me a bit and found out I would be partnering up with old Dr. Ezell in August. The next thing I knew, I had just got moved into my very first office when he shows up wanting a new pair of glasses so he can see better to hunt ducks. I didn't know squat about duck hunting at the time, did I, Dick?"

"Why Pack Rat, you were so wet behind the ears I thought about throwing you a towel."

"Brewwwhhhaahhaaa..." added Vernon.

"Anyway, your dad comes lumbering in, towering over everything in sight, generally making a nuisance of himself."

"Nuisance? Nuisance! Why you were so jittery, I knew you were gonna crawl under your exam chair." Pop was wearing one of his stupefied, surprised faces.

"The way you stormed into the place, I was afraid you were going to break something, like my refurbished Reichert Phoropter. I had hocked my soul to buy it so I could start my practice."

"I thought you said Ezell lent you his old one."

"What do you think my monthly rent check covered? Anyway, your daddy nearly knocked over the whole tray of phoropter lens while I was trying to figure out his prescription, with all his flailing around and wiggling in the chair. You would have thought I had a big baby on my hands till he started settling down and asking if I'd ever been duck hunting. The way he talked you'd have been convinced he was the world's greatest expert."

"I most certainly am too. Vernon, tell him. You know how I can always call the ducky-blats right into the decoys."

"Harrumph, bruh, I don' know 'bout dat, Dick. I think I'm da one dat calls 'em in – taught you everything I know."

"Ricky, listen to me. They don't know what they're talking about. So, your daddy, he starts running off at the mouth about duck hunting this, and duck hunting that, and I thought I had gotten hold of a real cuckoo. Then, out of the blue, he asks me if I'd like to go down to Santee with him to hunt some ducks. I told him I didn't own a duck gun. He said I could borrow one from him the first time out, but I'd have to go get a license, duck stamps, a pair of waders, and a box a duck loads. I didn't have two dimes to rub together back then, but next thing I knew, I was down at Pack's Landing staying in old man Pack's motel. We're not related, by the way. Different set of Packs."

Vernon said, "That motel was trying to sink into the swamp. Now it's tryin' to git Pack's brick ranch house out on th' point. The swamp eventually takes everything, brub, braaah. Remember the ole houseboat? Ricky, you know."

There were no remains of the original houseboat to be found anymore. I said, "I was trying to go to sleep with my head aiming downhill. On top of that, I was sharing a queen bed with Pop, and he was so heavy I kept rolling into him all night long. The snoring was incredible, too! I didn't get any sleep."

"Finish your story, Alva. Rick doesn't know what he's talking about. We don't snore, do we, Vee Bee?"

"You snore, Dick."

"Alva, just finish your little story."

"Ricky, here I was stuck in a little motel room with the two of them, never having done anything like that before. Next morning, they froze my ass off in a damn little metal boat before dawn. We didn't get any ducks that morning, *and* they made me do all the work hanging catfish lines. Then, they showed me where the old houseboat had sunk. And damn if something incredible didn't happen. Remember the trap door in the middle that could be opened so you could fish right there from the inside? The door had rotted away, leaving nothing but an open hole between the old pontoons. Low and behold, there were several mason jars of Vernon's moonshine floating in the hole. We cracked them open and drank them right then and there. Eventually, it didn't matter a damn that Pack's motel was sinking. Hell, we had a good time, didn't we, Vernon?"

"Yeah, we did. We got us some mallards that night over in the Brambles."

"That's right, Vee Bee. We parked the boat on that muddy little island way up in there, put on our waders, and waded out into the Brambles for the evening shoot. And what did Pack do?" Pop smirked.

"How could I forget? Breh, heh, heh."

"Let's not talk about that, Dick," pleaded Alva. "Ricky's too young for that kind of story."

Unfortunately for the doctor, that was fuel to flame for Pop. "Vee Bee, you fed us your famous tater-and-onion loaf with mallards and brown gravy. Alva really enjoyed loading up on all that greasy food, didn't he Vee Bee? Didn't he?"

"Ricky, don't listen to them," said Alva. It was apparent he was looking forward to the retelling, no matter what it cost him. "Dick, if you're gonna insist, then let me tell it. It happened to me, not you."

"Okay, but if you don't tell it right, we'll take over, won't we, Vee Bee?"

"I'm jus' glad it ain't never happened to me."

"Here I was, struggling out into the swamp in thin cheap-ass Japanese waders, frozen stiff. Your daddy went off to the left. Vernon went off to the right. We were all set up, and shooting time was coming along when suddenly it hit me." Alva paused dramatically and looked at me.

I realized he was waiting for me to say something. "What hit you?" Pop and Vernon burst out laughing.

"The green apple quick step."

"The what?" I asked. Having not heard the terminology before, I began to formulate what was coming.

"Vernon's white liquor from the mason jars and all the greasy food – it sort of began to percolate. It was almost shooting time. I knew if I tried to make my way back to the bank and get out of my waders, I'd ruin the shoot for Vernon and for your daddy. I had no choice but to stand there and fill my waders all the way down to my toes."

Vernon and Pop roared.

Horror stole over me as what Dr. Pack had said conjured up images the likes of which I hoped I never experienced. I dared to ask, "W-what did you do?"

"My toes were warm for a while."

More laughter. Now eyeglasses were lifted, and tears were being wiped away.

"I was wearing thick wool socks. After a bit, my feet started freezing again. All I could think about was having to peel out of those waders with the two of them hanging around. I began to think that the shoot would last forever, but finally, your daddy and Vernon came on back. I had no choice but to tell them what happened. They made me sit up front on the way back to Pack's motel and keep my waders cinched tight with Dick's belt to hold in the stink. At least I had fresh clothes waiting for me."

Pop crowed, "We wouldn't let him back in the room till he got cleaned up. We threw a bar of soap and a towel at him and sent him to the boat landing to strip down and take a bath."

"It was dark, and no one else was around. The water was *cold*. I wasn't about to try to salvage the ruined clothes, but I did rinse out the waders. They were expensive, fifteen bucks, one-seventh of my weekly salary. I threw the clothes away."

The dinnertime mirth finally subsided. I had picked clean the carcasses of a couple of wood ducks and of my ill-gotten heron. Here we were eating the same meal as the one that set off Alva's constitution, except for the addition of my strange bird. For a while, all I could think was, *please* don't ever let that happen to me. After mulling it over, I finally decided that there was a lesson in this. One can't control much of anything, not even one's own bodily functions at times, so laughing is a survival skill more potent than a gun. Or – *hind*sight is twenty-twenty.

🦆🦆🦆🦆🦆🦆🦆🦆🦆

As an aside, I did eventually have a similar experience. I used to scuba dive, and it happened in a formfitting neoprene rubber suit at fifty-eight feet deep under Lake Jocassee, South Carolina. At least my toes were warm. Embarrassment, humiliation, degradation, all those negative thoughts came to undermine my self-confidence. So, I laughed at myself along with everybody else. All was right again with the world.

"Yesterday is history, tomorrow is a mystery, today is God's gift,
that's why we call it the present."
~ Joan Rivers

| 21 |

Diorama

The last gifts my father and I traded were on Christmas Day of nineteen-ninety. He gave me a handcrafted skinning knife in a velvet-lined cedar box. A card was enclosed with the scrawled words, "If I can leave you nothing but a love of the outdoors, so be it!" Although I had always been included in Pop's wilderness escapades, it took many years of pondering before I truly understood the import of his words. The fact is seasons come and seasons go, while the human body gets stuck with the bill. He knew that axiom all too well. Pop had repeatedly tried to impress upon me that the world's wealth can never replace love – and life is transient.

There are many forms of love, but a love of the outdoors is synonymous with a love of the Creation. I believe my father would have been satisfied knowing that he had achieved this one thing in my life: to recognize something greater than myself and rejoice in it. Pop couldn't force me to believe in the Unseen Living God, but he could set my feet on a path to help me decide for myself that God exists. Only unconditional love could bring this wondrous world to teeming life in an otherwise stone-cold universe. We have all had the opportunity to experience this incredible miracle. Few of us have accepted what our senses tell us. There is a Plan.

Of all the types of people, I think outdoorsmen are probably the closest to God because of their love of His Creation. It takes patience to catch a fish or hunt the many tasty varieties of wild game. It also takes patience to understand the symbiosis between Man and the environment. Standing in waders for hours in freezing water, stock-still, holding a gun, hoping for at least one good shot at a zigzagging duck at dawn means you will either learn patience and become one with Nature – or quit. Real outdoorsmen never quit.

During all those trying moments, I was closest to the Plan. I could hear my own heartbeat, feel the chill-induced burning sensation in my extremities, flick the icicles of snot from my nostrils, know the excitement of a glorious sunrise, hear the inch-thick ice sigh as the warming rays intensified. One needs to encounter the Great Outdoors for oneself to truly grasp its wonder. Ah, but I wax poetic. Months earlier, I had decided to capture all this emotion in a gift for Pop. It took hope and prayer.

After all, he could buy almost anything he wanted, so he had everything. I had already given him too many neckties. He had a plethora of duck calls, camo, and hunting gear. I imagined he might like something different, something more meaningful. Pop's gift would have to be made from scratch.

Creating the gift required a trip to Santee specifically to gather authentic materials. I would need real cypress wood, some Spanish moss, and a bunch of 35mm camera photos to pull it off. As part of my childhood learning experience, Pop taught me how to build models of many types, including cars, boats, airplanes, and spaceships. Also, I had worked with balsa wood to create radio-controlled models. I decided to make a diorama of the houseboat, incorporating the most memorable aspects of Santee. Nothing I had made before even came close to what I wanted for Pop. For him, I tried to offer one last memory of all the good times we shared at Santee.

Through his fatherly love, Pop caused me to develop a deep appreciation for God and His Creation. I sincerely regret those times when I was a selfish, petulant child trying to make him think I wasn't enjoying our outdoor experiences. I wanted him to understand he succeeded in teaching me the things a man needs to know. Pop was not one to cry easily, but the surprise and tears that came will never be forgotten. The lighted diorama sat in a prominent place in his den where he could see it until his final days ten months later. I was glad it brought him a modicum of pleasure, and I thanked God for giving me the inspiration and talent to make the gift.

Two years earlier, in October of '89, Pop and I made what was to be our final trip to Santee. I didn't know it, and I don't think he did either. As with all the other trips, we were scouting ducks before the opening day of hunting season. The leaves on the cypress trees were adorned with autumn colors. Sunshine in the mid-afternoon warmed the textured waterscape invitingly. Turtles basked on every log, birds preened in the treetops, otters frolicked around every island of pigweed, beavers traversed sections of open water searching for edible morsels, squirrels chittered from on high, and even a

A Santee Golden Eagle
Photo courtesy of Michael Free, 2018

golden eagle scowled down from its nest on high. It was going to be a perfect, cloudless evening for watching ducks come to roost.

Pop found a log with multiple clumps of mossy limbs that would hide us effectively. He began to work the boat alongside. It was my job to push branches out of the way as we slipped into position. Pop joggled us side to side, gently plowing a path. I ducked under a particularly mossy limb and was confronted with a situation that nearly stopped my heart.

"*POP,*" I screamed. He didn't hear me over the roar of the motor as he operated the throttle. I screamed again.

He heard this time and immediately cut the motor. "What's wrong, Boy?"

"H-hornets," I managed to breathe out. Fear lanced through me. My back was flattened against my seat, my arms pushing limbs aside to prevent them from whipping the biggest, *baddest* nest of stinging bugs I had ever seen! I held my breath, trying not to brush against the horror. Thousands of black hornets clung to the gray paper surface, glistening in the sunlight.

Pop exclaimed, "My God!" He had seen my predicament. As always, he forced down his fear and, with a calm voice, said, "Hold whatcha got, Son. I'm gonna start the motor and back us out. It's gonna be rough and fast, so brace yourself so you don't fall forward. Got me?"

"Y-yes, sir." I wondered how I would keep those limbs in my hands from whipping that nest as we backed away.

"Here we go!"

Time stopped.

Pop threw it in reverse and gunned the throttle. I could hear water flooding over the transom. The boat slid backward so fast the limbs were wrenched out of my hands. In slow motion, I saw them whip into that four-foot-high upside-down cone – and bust a basketball-sized hole in its surface. Obviously taken by surprise, black bodies spilled out, covering the surface immediately below the nest like an oil slick.

Pop backed the boat off fifty feet or so and cut the motor again. I was shaking so bad I had to put my head between my knees and take a breather.

"Rick, would you look at that." Whenever Pop used my proper name, I knew it was important. I forced my head up.

Never had I seen such a sight. From the shadows where the hornet's nest hung, a dark cyclone was rising into the air. It mushroomed just above the treetop and became a black, swirling cloud of stinging terrors. As we watched, awed to silence, the mass bent toward the declining sun and whipped away.

The only time I had ever seen anything similar was on Hanna-Barbara's Yogi Bear cartoon. I always figured the television show had to get the idea somewhere. Adrenalin slipped away as fast as it had come, leaving me weak. I had never giggled, but now I couldn't stop myself. Pop joined in with full-bellied laughter. I turned around to face him, and we spent a good five minutes clearing our systems before we could speak.

"Boy, was that a close call or what?"

"Pop, don't ever do that to me again."

"What? What'd I do?"

"You're the captain, right?"

"Right."

"The captain makes all the decisions, accepts all the consequences for his actions, and goes down with the ship if necessary. Next time, I'm driving!"

He grinned sheepishly. "You're right, Boy, I am the captain. And the captain says you need a drink! Now, get me the bottle of Jack, and I'll fix you right up! You've earned it!"

He was right. I had earned it. We sat there sharing the first adult beverage we ever drank together as the woodies flew in with the waning light. The swamp stilled. All the animals went to their nocturnal homes except for the great owl above our heads hooting for its mate.

"I offer a toast," Pop said in a subdued tone, "to my son. He's a chip off the old block. He's made me proud in uncounted ways. I've done my best to keep him straight. Like fathers everywhere, we want our sons to be better men than ourselves. My goal has been achieved. I know that Richard Carl Meehan, Jr. will carry on the tradition. To you, my son."

Wise Old Santee Owl

I couldn't see through my now fogged yellow shooting glasses. But I did manage to say, "I'm proud to have you as my dad."

Yes, I really did tell him before he died. So many never get the opportunity to say that to a parent. The time never seems right. As I removed my glasses and looked out across the dark water, I knew I had done something extraordinary. I had made Pop happy.

Darkness overtook us at last, just as it was designed to do. We headed back to the houseboat for supper and our customary time stargazing and relaxing on the porch. Once more, the timeless nature of Santee pressed upon me.

"Boy, tell me something. Just how did you do it?"

Instantly I knew what he was asking. "I was looking at her hooters, Pop."

Luna, my goddess of old, rose in full glory, beckoning, cajoling, luring us to come and join her, one day, in the Grand Scheme of Eternity. I felt like a man.

Duck Tale

"You can go home now, Dicky. The battle is over. Just rest, my love."
~ *Mommy*

22

Pop's Farewell

Wars rage across cerebral plains,
drug-driven to stem the pains.
Where once a boisterous man trod,
left now only a husk to prod.

Duck Tale

Cancerous Nature expands,
pray for God's healing hands.

Push the button of Relief,
wash your system with the Thief.

Thief of Body, thief of Soul,
morphine, morphine, here we go.

Greedy little men like Watchers sit,
beside your bed to give you a fit.

From one horror to another,
never a sound do they utter.

Beneath the Watchers' gaze battles rage,
against an unseen horrid phage.

No quarter were the soldiers giving,
only blows to steal your living.

Concerned they are with not a thing,
except to destroy all you've gained.

Picking at Life itself,
they rend and tear at your health.

The blood-borne Armies have won,
the war, however, still goes on.

Men, women, and children die,

by Leukemia turning cells awry.

One thing was your life worth,
a sacrifice deemed upon your birth.

That medical science might advance a step,
though your family and friends wept.

Emptiness is all your eyes hold now,
where before there was a Great Will.

Eternal peace is yours at last,
rest now far from the Watcher's grasp.

Appendix

Favorite Wild Game Recipes
Preparation

Usually when someone tells me they don't eat wild game they cite the ethereal gamey flavor. So, how do you get rid of this distasteful turnoff? It's easy. Here is a tip that works for all wild game:

1. Put the wild meat, whether fish, bird, or beast, into a pot or bowl large enough to allow it to be filled with water until the meat is covered.
2. Add a generous helping of salt. About a quarter cup per gallon should be sufficient.
3. Add half a cup of white vinegar per gallon.
4. Agitate until the salt is dissolved.
5. Allow the meat to soak in the refrigerator overnight. This will remove excess blood, tenderize, and remove the gamey flavor from the meat.
6. Drain the solution and rinse the meat in clear water thoroughly.
7. That's it. You're done. Go make a delectable wild game dish. If you don't have a favorite recipe, use one of mine. I guarantee you'll have a main course fit for royalty.

Ricky's Authentic Santee Catfish Stew

Ingredients:

    3 - 4 pounds of fresh caught Santee Cats, skin removed, or farm-raised catfish (if you must)
    2 large Idaho potatoes, diced, or 2 cans of diced potatoes
    2 - 8 oz. cans sliced mushrooms (optional, but I love 'em)
    1 can sweet yellow corn
    1 can diced tomatoes
    1 small Vidalia onion, chopped
    1 tbsp. butter
    1 tsp. Old Bay Seasoning
    1 tbsp. Worcestershire Sauce
    1 tbsp. Frank's Hot Sauce

1/2 tbsp. Pepper (fresh ground is best)
1 tbsp. salt (sea salt is best)
1 qt. milk (whole or skim)
2 cans Carnation Brand condensed milk

Directions:

1. Sauté onions in butter until caramelized.
2. Add all seasons while onions are cooking.
3. Add fish and vegetables. If canned vegetables, use the liquid too.
4. Add water to cover and bring to boil until fish breaks apart.
5. Once fish is falling apart add all milk.
6. Stir gently once milk is added and bring to serving temperature. DO NOT BOIL.
7. Add further salt and pepper to taste if desired.

Recommendations:

Ricky's Authentic Santee Catfish Stew is best when served on the second day, but you don't have to wait. Freshly prepared will still knock your socks off! Preparation time: one hour.

Appendix

Brad's Bodacious Doves with Potato Loaf

Ingredients:

    10 - 12 Wild Doves, whole (or substitute 8 – 10 quail)
    2 - 3 large Idaho potatoes, sliced 1/4" thick
    2 - 3 large Vidalia onions, sliced 1/4" thick
    1 cup fresh black coffee
    1 cup flour
    4 tbsp. vegetable oil
    1 tbsp. fresh garlic, minced
    1 stick butter, sliced into pats
    Salt
    Pepper

Directions:

1. Mix flour in bowl with heavy salt and pepper (to taste) and set aside.
2. Make fresh coffee and set aside.
3. Place potatoes and onions in a loaf pan, covering liberally with salt and pepper.
4. Lay pats of butter on top of potatoes and onions.
5. Spread garlic across top of potatoes and onions.
6. Bake loaf at 350 degrees for 30 minutes. Cover with aluminum foil and cook another 15 minutes until done.
7. When potato loaf is nearly done, heat oil in large iron skillet.
8. Lay doves in hot oil and fry both sides until meat is tender.
9. Mix coffee and flour thoroughly until uniform.
10. Pour flour mixture quickly into skillet.
11. Stir gently to create dark brown gravy surrounding doves. Should be thick.

Recommendations:

Brad's Bodacious Doves with Potato Loaf is best served immediately upon completion of the gravy. Place serving of potato loaf in middle of plate, then add several whole doves. Ladle gravy over top. Preparation time: 1.5 hours. Serves 4-6 depending on how many doves per person. Usually, three doves for each person are sufficient, unless you're as big as Pop.

Note: When substituting quail, one or two birds per person are sufficient. Add frying time because of the larger sized bird.

Vee Bee's Venerable Santee Wood Ducks Over Wild Rice

Ingredients:

- 2 - 5 Wild Ducks (one for each person)
- 2 - 3 large Idaho potatoes, sliced thick
- 2 - 3 large Vidalia onions, sliced thick
- 1 cup fresh hot black coffee
- Salt (cover outside of birds liberally and sprinkle potatoes and onions)
- Pepper (lots of it on the birds and some on the potatoes and onions)
- Long grain wild rice (prepared separately for number of servings required)
- 1 - 2 cans jellied cranberry sauce, chilled

Appendix

Directions:

Using a large pressure cooker (or steamer pot with basket):

1. Make sure bottom strainer is inserted in pressure cooker.
2. Pour in fresh black coffee (removes gamey taste)
3. Place potatoes and onions in bottom.
4. Place ducks on top of potatoes and onions.
5. Apply salt and pepper as described above. Vee Bee used lots of pepper.
6. Once pressure cooker is up to temperature, cook for 20 minutes.

Recommendations:

Vee Bee's Venerable Santee Wood Ducks are best served over wild long grain rice with several side slices of chilled jellied cranberry sauce. Preparation time: 45 minutes. Serves 4-5, but this depends on how many ducks and vegetables you can fit in the pressure cooker.

Alva Pack Rat's Delectable Santee Duck Gumbo

Ingredients:

- 2 - 3 Wild Ducks depending on size or 3-4 Coots
- 2 bay leaves
- 1 clove garlic, minced
- 3 ribs celery, chopped
- 1 large Vidalia onion, chopped
- 1 large bell pepper, chopped
- 1 lb. okra, chopped
- 1 (3/4 oz pkg) brown gravy mix
- 1 tbsp. vegetable oil
- 1 lb. can whole tomatoes

1 tbsp. cracked black pepper
1 tbsp. parsley flakes
1/2 tbsp. Worcestershire sauce
Juice of 1/2 lemon
1 tbsp. gumbo filé powder (ground sassafras root)
Salt to taste
Tabasco brand sauce to taste
White rice, cooked

Directions:

1. Cover ducks* with water and boil with bay leaves until tender.
2. Remove meat from bones and chop (discard bones.) SAVE THE BROTH.
3. Add garlic, celery, onion, bell pepper and okra to broth.
4. In another pan make roux (gumbo base) using gravy mix or left-over stir-fry broth.
5. Add tomatoes and pepper to roux, then mix with saved broth.
6. Add parsley and meat and simmer 2 ½ to 3 hours, stirring often.
7. Add Tabasco brand sauce, Worcestershire brand sauce, lemon juice, salt and filé powder.

Recommendations:

Alva Pack Rat's Delectable Santee Duck Gumbo is best served over tender white rice. Preparation time: 3 hours. Serves 4-5.

*If using coots, stir fry them in ½ cup of vegetable oil, ¼ stick of butter, ¼ cup orange marmalade, and ¼ cup old coffee (removes wild taste). When making the roux, use the stir-fry broth from frying the coots instead of water.

David's Sweet 'n Easy Cobbler

Ingredients:

One 10" cast iron Dutch oven (or deep casserole dish)
Two cans pie filling (Apple, Peach, Cherry, etc.)
One box yellow cake mix
Cool Whip or Vanilla Ice Cream
Bag of charcoal briquettes

Directions:

1. For a 10" Dutch oven, gather 22 briquettes, pile them together, and light to burn until they form the slight ashy coating and are ready for use.

Appendix

2. Line the Dutch oven with either a store-bought disposable liner or plain aluminum foil, to make cleanup easier.
3. In a bowl, combine half the box of mix with half of the recommended amount of water (for the full box), plus about another ¼ cup water. Don't add any eggs, oil, etc. Larger Dutch ovens will take more mix to cover the fruit.
4. Pour the cans of pie filling in the bottom of the Dutch oven, and pour the batter mixture on top, and place the oven lid on.
5. Place 8 coals in a small symmetrical circle under the Dutch oven (to heat from below), and the remaining 14 coals on top of the lid (to bake from above) in a symmetrical pattern.
6. Cook for approx. 45 minutes, turning the oven ninety degrees one way and the lid ninety degrees the other way, every fifteen minutes, to allow for even heat.
7. Check for doneness by testing the cake for fluffiness and a golden-brown color. Remove from heat and enjoy!

Recommendations:

No Santee wild game meal is complete without a Dutch oven dessert to finish. This simple recipe can be made anywhere, and most any fruit works well. Store-bought pie fillings are simple and easy to use. Nothing beats a hot bowl of apple cobbler with ice cream after a hearty wild game dinner!

Biographies

Although it is customary for biographical information to be written in "third person," I am giving leeway to this rule to allow several of the characters to compose in their own words.

Dr. Alva S. Pack, III

I was born July 19, 1943, in Greenville, South Carolina, delivered by my grandfather, Dr. Alva S. Pack Sr. My mother and I lived with my dad's family while Dad served in WWII. He was injured in the D-Day Invasion and was transferred to an Army Air Corp Hospital in Orlando, Florida. We moved to be with him. I was a year old.

Dad had no ambition to be a doctor, lawyer, or Indian chief, and was a butcher at an A & P grocery store. We lived on a dirt road a few miles from the store, so he rode his bicycle to work until his dad bought him a car. I was in first grade then. Dad hunted and fished, not for the sport of it, but for the food of it. At six, I had my first BB gun and would shoot doves off the power lines, which was illegal of course, and squirrels in the trees so we could have meat on the table.

All good things usually end at some time. My turn came when I was in third grade. We lost our home, my parents divorced, and my mom, sister, and I moved in with her mother. When Grandmother died, we moved to government housing.

I got a work permit at age 14 and my first real job at the A & P grocery as a bag boy. I worked, but not to buy things. I helped pay for the rent, food, utilities, etc., to help Mom. I kept my tip money to buy clothes, a deer rifle, fishing gear, Coca-Colas, and M&Ms. For six years I worked for A & P, through high school and junior

Appendix

college. Between work and studies, I found time to do a little hunting and fishing. My BB gun days on that dirt road taught me to love the outdoors, put food on the table, and to eat what I killed – Hunter's Rule #1.

When I moved to Spartanburg in June 1969, I was turning 26 and had three degrees: an A.A., B.S., and an O.D. I made some lifelong friends in the Jaycees. My best friend was Dick Meehan.

At 77, I still hunt and fish, but over the past twelve years, while Dr. Louis Martin and his wife, Dr. Janell Martin have been buying out my fifty-year-old Optometry practice, I hit the books again. I now hold a B.A. from the University of South Carolina Upstate.

My four children's ages range from 41-53 and my ten grandchildren from 2-26. All the above live in four different states. Needless to say, my wife, Janice, and I travel a lot.

Friends and family have passed, but sunrises and sunsets continue every day, and hopefully too our memories as represented in this book.

Alva holding a big catfish

Appendix

Dick, My Friend

You taught me as a young Jaycee,
You taught me how to love Santee,
You taught me how to turkey hunt,
You taught me about the Edisto muck.
You helped me through problems with my first wife,
You were the best man for the woman of my life.
You were always there when I needed a friend,
We were together when we needed to say Amen.
Your companionship has been missed these past years,
You and I both had to learn to overcome our fears.
You will be missed dearly by family and friends,
But your memory will be forever as the wind.
You will be in the Autumn leaves that fall,
Your voice will be heard in every duck call.
You will be as the winter mist on a pond,
Even though your body and soul are far beyond.
You will be part of each blade of grass in the Spring,
As refreshing as every new raindrop God brings.
You will be in each summer sunset and sunrise,
And in the old Santee owl who is so wise.
You will be in my heart each and every day,
So I may learn the meaning of Life along the way.
Goodbye my friend,
We will see each other again.

~ Alva

This poem was given as the eulogy at Pop's funeral.

Vernon E. Burnett (1932-2016)

Born January 12, 1932, in Spartanburg, South Carolina, raised on Edward Avenue, Vernon Burnett was the son of the late Robert Henry and Ruth Toney Burnett. Vernon became an Eagle Scout and was inducted into the Order of the Arrow. He was a National Guard veteran. Later in life he achieved the rank of Master Mason with the Glendale Masonic Lodge. His profession was Electrician, and he served in machine maintenance with Pepsi-Cola of Spartanburg, followed by the S. C. School for the Deaf and Blind until retirement. For many years he repaired guns in his spare time from his backyard shop.

Vernon graduated from Spartanburg High School. He was a member of Glendale Baptist Church where he served as a deacon for many years. Roberta Bradley Burnett, his wife of sixty-three years, passed on March 31, 2020. He always referred to her and the other hunters' wives as the "duck widows." Roberta was a saint.

As a young boy, Vernon was introduced to hunting by a neighbor. From that point he would take his shotgun on the bus to school and walk home to hunt along the railroad tracks. Although his parents did not hunt, his mother would always cook anything he brought home. With the rise of subdivisions, the farms and fields he hunted as a boy gradually disappeared.

One of his favorite pastimes was watching ducks lighting in the decoys. He spent many hours practicing his duck calling with his friend Dick, whom he had met by chance (or Providence) in the late '60's down at Sparkleberry Landing, Rimini, S.C. It was the beginning of a tight friendship that eventually included Alva Pack, described herein as The Three Duck-kateers. This is an apt description of their relationship.

Vernon took great pleasure in hunting and fishing during all seasons with his friends, but most especially because he was accompanied by his son, Brad, and later his grandchildren. His favorite gun was a Winchester Model 12 pump action shotgun, but once regulations changed to eliminate the use of lead shot, his choice gun for duck hunting was a Benelli Super Black Eagle. It could be loaded with three-point-five-inch-long magnum loads with No. 4 steel shot, which made up for the difference between superior lead shot and lighter stainless steel.

Each year at Christmastime, in his capacity as a Master Mason, Vernon would make his rounds to visit the wives of deceased friends. He would always carry a small gift such as flowers or candy or a basket of fresh fruit. His words upon arrival to see Dick's wife, Ann, were always "I've brought a little something for the widows…harrumph." He would give a sincere, close-lipped smile, and a warm hug.

Vernon in hunting mode

Vernon "Brad" Burnett

Brad was born on September 14, 1956, in Spartanburg, South Carolina. He graduated from Pacolet High school and went on the get a B.S. in Computer Programming from USC-Spartanburg (now USC-Upstate). He worked for the J. M. Smith Corporation for 41 years until he retired in 2020. Brad married his second wife, Debbie, on June 10th, 2000, and his son, Colten, was born on Aug 27th, 2002. When Colten was twelve, he asked to go to Boy Scouts, so Brad got them both involved with local Troop 603, Blue Ridge Council. Brad went through Woodbadge leadership training so he could become an Assistant Scout Master and be involved with his son's troop. He enjoyed taking the boys camping, and although his son is grown and out of the house, Brad continues as a Scout leader.

Brad was brought up hunting and fishing from a very early age. With his father running a gun repair shop, Brad was always testing the guns. If he could hold it (with help), he would shoot it. He began hunting with his father at six years old. When he was eight, he received an Ithaca 20-gauge single barrel shotgun for hunting doves and ducks. His father took him to Sparkleberry Landing, Rimini, S.C. later that year to camp and duck hunt. It was the first time he could stand on his own at the edge of a swamp holding a gun without adult supervision. This was considered a major honor and achievement for a young boy. It meant that he had the maturity to use his weapon responsibly. The next year Brad had grown into shooting a double barrel 12-gauge.

When he turned ten, Brad received a Winchester Model 12 pump action shotgun for Christmas. His father took him duck hunting and he got his first duck with that gun. It was a wood duck. The woodie was mounted by a taxidermist and still hangs on Brad's living room wall. "My father and I hunted regularly with the Meehans and Alva Pack for many years. Although I have not been to Santee for more than a quarter of a century, I still cherish the memories of those incredible and rewarding times."

Vernon (left), Brad (right) after a successful hunt

Appendix

David W. Atherton

Born in Spartanburg, South Carolina on September 23, 1960, David was the youngest of three sons to Richard "Dick" and Louise Atherton. David graduated from Spartanburg High School in 1978, attended Furman University, but transferred to the University of South Carolina in Columbia where, in 1983, he received a B.S. in Business Administration.

David's father, a career electrician, opened Atherton Electric Co. in the late 1950s. David and his brothers worked for Dick during the summers. While David's brothers went on to other careers after college, he remained in Spartanburg, continuing to work with his father for many years, eventually becoming the CEO after his father's decline in health. Through good times and bad, they were able to make a decent living to support their family until the economy declined during the 2000's. David sold the business in 2008.

In college, David became interested in the military, went through ROTC, and graduated as a 2nd Lieutenant, and continued to a parallel career in the S.C. Army National Guard in Field Artillery and Air Defense Artillery, retiring as a Lt. Colonel after 28 years of service.

His mother, Louise, taught deaf children at the S.C. School for the Deaf and Blind. She also managed to care for the family, while Dick slaved away creating and growing his contracting business as David was growing up. Neither of his parents had any hobbies or enjoyable pastimes other than working, so as a young squirt, he felt very fortunate to have become pals with Rick Meehan in junior high school, a friendship that has continued to this day.

After watching his parents work constantly and not take pleasure from hobbies or vacations, David resolved not to become locked into endless work. He was married to Sharon Robbins of Charleston, S.C. in 1984, also a schoolteacher, and eventually took over his father's business. He has three fabulous children who are all now grown and gone their separate ways: Greg, Steven, and Kelly.

Guns, boats, hunting, fishing, and military have all been a large part of his life, and he is proud to have lived through so many varied adventures with family and friends. Some of those experiences can be voiced, but others must remain secret. This book lets the reader peek in on a few of those stories best told around a campfire with close friends.

David with wife, Sharon, at Santee

Appendix

Duck Hunting

Here it is, dark and cold
Getting up early sure does get old.
I'm in the swamp, my gun in my hand.
I would rather be at home dreaming of La La Land.
The morning is quiet, the day is still
And all this ice is giving me a chill.
Suddenly I hear a familiar sound.
I see the ducks, and my heart starts to pound.
I see the ducks coming my way
I shoulder my gun and blast away.
Their wings fold, their heads drop,
And hit the water with a resounding "WOP"!
But wait! That bird is still splashing
I know he is doomed
But my brother says,
"I got 'im! BOOM! BOOM! BOOM!"
The duck in the water is floating along.
I whistle a tune, a victorious song.
I waddle over to get my bird
A Kodak moment worth a thousand words.

Steven Atherton enjoyed the moment and found inspiration to write this poem

Richard "Dick" Carl Meehan (1937 – 1991)

Dick was born in Pottsville, Pennsylvania on November 26, 1937, to the late Evelyn Beachum Meehan Boyette and Franklin Meehan. While growing up, he spent much time helping on his grandparent's farm (Beachum) in Anson County, North Carolina. In 1959, he graduated from the University of North Carolina at Chapel Hill with a B.S. in Chemistry.

He was a Boy Scout leader, Jaycee, Mason, Shriner, and Lion. Dick was also highly involved in Duck's Unlimited, Harry Hampton Memorial Wildlife Fund, and the South Carolina Waterfowler's Association.

Dick married Ann Crichton Breedlove on August 16, 1959. They had two children, Ricky and Melanie. In 1968, Dick and Ann formed Marko Chemical Co., Inc., a producer of quality cleaning detergents and supplier of sanitation paper, equipment, and machines.

Somehow, between running Marko and being involved in all the civic activities, he found time to attend his childrens' programs which included karate, baseball, basketball, Scouting and band, sometimes as a leader or coach. Every July Fourth week he would take the family on vacations. In addition, he traversed the State with his friends, hunting and fishing. He was rarely idle. As an avid reader, his tastes included thrillers, spy novels, historical fiction, the *Foxfire* series, and finance. His favorite outdoor activity was bird hunting, so he collected guns, duck calls, turkey calls, and knives. Much time was spent seeking new places to hunt, but Santee became his favorite.

After several years of struggle against leukemia, he succumbed on October 2, 1991, at the age of 53. His company is still run by his wife and family at the time of this writing. His son and daughter enjoy the outdoors, passing along his legacy to his grandchildren.

Pop demonstrating how to catfish using drop lines in '76

Acknowledgments

To K. Gail McAbee, author extraordinaire, mentor, and inspiration by your very presence, I thank you from the depths of my being for your gracious support over many years. Likewise, to your husband, Jerry, for his relevant commentary.

To Brad Burnett, a real hunter who learned from the best, may these stories that intertwined our lives bring satisfaction that all is not forgotten, and that the good times really were.

To Vernon E. Burnett, in memoriam, I'll never forget your strong but gentle nature, your unswerving friendship to my father, and your down-to-earth wisdom.

To Dr. Alva S. Pack, III, your friendship and support were highly valued by my father. He constantly related your exploits in travel, business, marriage, children, re-marriage, children, amazing spirit, and humor to me as an example of living life to the fullest.

To Janice Pack, your editorial skills were most appreciated, as they helped make my efforts worthy of the public eye.

To David W. Atherton, my friend during times dark and light, my companion who grew alongside me under the wings of the Great Hunter, my father. Thank you for beta reading this project and offering editorial advice.

To Larry D. Shull, words alone cannot say all that needs to be said. Please know that your righteous spirit has been as a beacon lighting the path to Glory.

To Trace and Edie Miller, I appreciate your critical eyes and suggestions. They helped make this work the best it can be.

To Steve and Sherry Hoffman, it was a leap of faith to delve into the rough draft and take a swim. I appreciate your laughing, contemplating, and crying in all the right places.

To my wife, Renee, for listening patiently with a critical ear, repeatedly. The red marks of your mighty pen surely made this book an easier read. What would one expect from a teacher?

To all of those who once called Dick Meehan a friend, and to all the supporters of wildlife conservation here in South Carolina, and the world, please continue to back the cause so future generations may enjoy the incredible beauty of our precious wetlands.

Also Available

ALSO AVAILABLE BY RICHARD C. MEEHAN, JR.

The Thing in the Tub: *Power Dreams* ~ poems for children
Port Nowhere: *The Charlie Manus thread* ~ sci-fi anthology
Omega Station: *Charlie Manus thread (cont.)* ~ sci-fi anthology
Cometary Tales: *Short Story Collection* ~ sci-fi book
The Janitor's Closet: *Cleaning Industry* ~ a business "how to"

COMING SOON:
Ford the Pacholet: *A Revolutionary War historical fiction novel*

Richard Carl Meehan, Jr.

I was born in Charlotte, North Carolina on July 18, 1960. In 1963, my family moved to Spartanburg, South Carolina. Richard Sr., Pop, founded Marko Chemical Co., Inc. in 1968, and proceeded to build the company into a leading supplier of janitorial products. The foundation of Pop's business was his personally formulated Marko brand cleaning detergent line, quality soaps for all types of tough jobs.

From the beginning, I was known as the S.O.B. (son-of-boss). Pop started me off right, mowing the grass with a sling blade. I was eight. Nothing much happened while I was growing up unless you consider what I've written in this book, or my hands-on experience manufacturing and packaging detergents every summer vacation from the time I was knee high to a grasshopper. I nearly shortened my legs with that sling blade, but the grasshopper got away.

As I grew older, manual labor became an after-school pastime. Pop was all for teaching a good work ethic. My mistake came when I learned to type, not "keyboarding," but real live typing on an authentic Royal manual typewriter at Spartanburg High School. That's when my mother, Ann Breedlove Meehan, got a grip on me. She ran the office at Marko. Mommy discovered that I was good at processing sextuplicate forms and erasing errors on all carbon copies of the same, as necessary, every day after band practice. Eventually she discovered that I could crank the adding machine to figure salesmen's commissions to the penny. Meanwhile my teachers always complemented my term papers. I never stopped writing although I now prefer to use a computer instead of having to slam the carriage return after every line.

Then I went off to Wofford College, all the way across town, in 1978. That's where I learned about how money flows and got my B.A. in Economics. Despite that, English Lit was my favorite subject.

On graduation day, Pop shook my hand, said "congratulations" and told me that I would start work as a salesman on Monday morning at 8:00

A.M. sharp. I knew nothing about selling anything to anyone, but protestations never worked in my family. My mantra became, "Come rain nor shine nor sleet nor snow, the Marko Man is always on the go," and *go* I did. Mommy still runs the show too (at the time of this writing).

Over many years I have written opinion columns, how-to articles, short stories, children's poems, Christian literature, and personal essays for local newspapers, national magazines, websites, blogs, and e-zines. However, my favorite genre is science fiction. An avid fan, I enjoy reading about and imagining strange places, odd beings, and future tech, with the hopes that one day I might describe something which eventually becomes a commonplace tool. I doubt that a shotgun shell wood duck whistle will foot the bill, but something along the lines of a cell phone would be pretty cool. Surely all those sunsets on the porch at the houseboat helped my imagination.

I have spent my life garnering knowledge of one type or another, hands on, sleeves rolled up. Although my hats have changed many times over the years, I live by the motto put forth by Pop: "Learn something new every single day." I also added, "… and read." As should be obvious by now, I believe Pop was right to take me along on hunting trips with his amazing friends, to teach me how to work, and to never be a bench warmer. Now, *go* and do likewise.

**Rick and his Remington
1100 in 1980**

In Remembrance

Parts of The Boat

www.ingramcontent.com/pod-product-compliance
Lightning Source LLC
Chambersburg PA
CBHW072223200426
43209CB00073B/1928/J